1016 & 1066

WHY THE VIKINGS CAUSED
THE NORMAN CONQUEST

1016 & 1066

WHY THE VIKINGS CAUSED THE NORMAN CONQUEST

Martyn and Hannah Whittock

ROBERT HALE

First published in 2016 by Robert Hale,
an imprint of The Crowood Press Ltd,
Ramsbury, Marlborough, Wiltshire SN8 2HR

www. crowood.com

www.halebooks.com

British Library Cataloguing-in-Publication Data
A catalogue record for this book is available from the British Library.

ISBN 978 0 7198 1919 3

Dedication
To Ben Gunstone and Steve Dudley, as a reminder of all our history
discussions, including those in the rain and mud!

Typeset by Jean Cussons Typesetting, Diss, Norfolk

Printed and bound in India by Replika Press Pvt Ltd

Contents

Introduction

The Norman Conquest of 1066 is indelibly impressed on the history and the public awareness of England and, indeed, the whole of the United Kingdom because it was to eventually impact on the whole of the British Isles. Yet it was not the only 'Conquest' in the eleventh century. Exactly fifty years earlier, in 1016, England had experienced a 'Viking Conquest'. It is the contention of this book that it was this 'Viking Conquest' in 1016 that, more than any other factor, led to the much more famous 'Norman Conquest' of 1066. In short: the Vikings caused the Norman Conquest.

Since this book explores events of the eleventh century in England, Scandinavia and Normandy (with a brief excursion to Hungary), there are some issues that may benefit from a brief explanation at this point.

Language

The evidence from the eleventh century was written in the following languages: Old English, Latin, Norman-French and Old Norse. In the case of Old Norse, while it was spoken in various forms and dialects across the Viking world it has left fewer written examples from the period in question than the others; this is because literacy came much later to Scandinavia than to other areas of Western Europe. It does not always seem like this because a number of dramatic Old Norse written sources survive (most notably the sagas), which claim to shed light on this period. However, many of these sources date from a century or more after the events they describe and many were written in Iceland. Their evidence needs to be used with caution.

Whenever we quote from a source in these languages we always do so in a modern translation. The exception is when there is something note-worthy about a particular word or phrase that stands out as evidence. In that case we refer to it in the original language and translate it in order to explain it.

Old English and Old Norse used letters that are no longer used in Modern English. The most commonly used ones were: Æ or lowercase æ (ash), Ð or lowercase ð (eth) and Þ or lowercase þ (thorn). The last two approximated to the 'th' sound in modern English. The one we have employed when referring to personal names is Æ/æ because it was so commonly used and does not have a direct parallel in modern English.

For this reason we refer to Æthelred, not Ethelred. However, where a name has become more familiar in a modernized form, we have used the modern appearance; therefore, for example, we refer to Alfred not Ælfred.

Elsewhere, we have only rarely used these letters when a word or phrase quoted in the original language uses them. An example would be the Anglo-Scandinavian word *lið* (seaborne military), which was used in the *Anglo-Saxon Chronicle* to describe both the forces of the Anglo-Saxon Harold Godwinson's sons and those of Svein Estrithson of Denmark after 1066. Another example is the Old English word *ætheling* (prince, throne-worthy royal); we refer to the *æthelings* Edward and Alfred when discussing two Anglo-Saxon princes who were in exile in Normandy, and Edgar *ætheling* is the usual way that this prince is identified.

Anglo-Saxon … English … England

The people living in England before the Norman Conquest described themselves as 'English', living in 'England' (albeit using the Old English versions of these terms). These were catch-all labels that summed up the amalgamation of regional groups and recently settled Scandinavians who, together, constituted one political community under one king of England. The term 'Anglo-Saxon' had been coined over a century earlier but was not the usual term used at the time. However, we use it today in order to identify this particular period of history. As such, it remains a useful label and we deploy it alongside 'English', particularly when we need to differentiate between those who had been part of the population for several centuries, in contrast to Danes and Norwegians (and the occasional Swede) who had settled more recently.

Personal names

Many of the personal names of the time can be spelled in more than one way, for three main reasons. The first is that at the time there was inconsistency; for example, 'Harold' is the same name as 'Harald'. This is complicated by the fact that the same names existed in England and Scandinavia and could be spelled differently in the two areas. 'Svein', for example, is the same name as 'Swein' and 'Swayne'. The second reason is that eleventh-century names used the letters mentioned above and so can be spelled in various ways in Modern English. The third reason is that fashions change in how later writers represent these ancient names. So, Danish 'Knutr' is more likely today to be spelled in an English form 'Cnut' but was often written as 'Canute' in the past. We have adopted a consistent pattern so that 'Cnut' is used of both rulers with that name and 'Svein' is used of the various men with that name. The exception is that we refer to Harold Godwinson (also known as Harold II) who became king of England in 1066 but Harald Hardrada of Norway who was killed by him in 1066. This is now quite a common convention and makes it easier to differentiate them. In the same way and for the same reason we refer to Harald Harefoot, the son of Cnut (also known as Harald I).

Two powerful and influential women were both called Ælfgifu. Emma of Normandy took this name after she married Æthelred II and before she later married Cnut; and Cnut's first wife was Ælfgifu of Northampton. To have two such significant women (both eventually married to Cnut) carrying the same name makes for confusion so we always call them Emma and Ælfgifu. We never refer to Emma as Ælfgifu.

Harold II Godwinson married two women named Edith but both played relatively minor roles in the events we describe; therefore we have not differentiated them other than by calling the first one Edith 'Swanneck', since this by-name was used by contemporaries.

We have also used other by-names, when they exist, as a way of differentiating people. As a consequence, we usually use the full names of Harold Godwinson and Harald Hardrada in order to differentiate them and we call Harold Godwinson's predecessor as king of England Edward 'the Confessor' to avoid confusion with Edward 'the Exile'. This does run the risk of making these by-names sound like surnames, which they were not, as some were only used by some people at the time and then only sometimes. And others were coined later. But this is a small price worth paying if it reduces confusion for modern readers.

Titles of medieval sources of evidence

We have used the titles of medieval written sources in their original language although, on the first occasion of use, we have also given their titles in translation, in order to explain the meaning. Thereafter we tend to use a shortened form of the original-language title. An example would be the *Encomium Emmae Reginae* (*In Praise of Queen Emma*) which, after the first use, is thereafter simply referred to as the *Encomium Emmae* or the *Encomium*. This is because it has become customary to use its original title, rather than the title in translation. Other examples are the *Vita Ædwardi Regis* (*Life of King Edward*) and William of Jumièges' *Gesta Normannorum Ducum* (*Deeds of the Norman Dukes*). In a similar way, where Old Norse sources are usually now referred to by their Old Norse name, we have continued to do so; for example *Heimskringla* (*Circle of the World*), the great saga history of Norwegian Viking kings. It also means that, should readers come across these sources in other studies, they will recognize them from these frequently used titles. Other source-names, though, are modern inventions and so only appear in modern form; an obvious example is the *Anglo-Saxon Chronicle*, which after its first use in any chapter we then just call the *Chronicle*.

Acknowledgements

We are grateful to our agent, Robert Dudley, and to Robert Hale and Crowood for their help and support in the commissioning of and the production of this book. Peter Bull, of Peter Bull Art Studio, produced the maps with a speed and flexibility that was much appreciated. We are also indebted to the historians, whose explorations of events and interpretations regarding their significance we have consulted. Hannah's studies in the department of Anglo-Saxon, Norse and Celtic (ASNC) at Cambridge University (both as an undergraduate and then in an MPhil year) provided a great many insights, which assisted in the exploration of the evidence and its interpretation. All errors, of course, are our own.

Martyn and Hannah Whittock

CHAPTER 1

'1066 And All That': So What?

A date to remember

In thirty-three years of teaching History in secondary schools one of the authors has frequently asked students to discuss with their families three key events in English history for which they can offer a date. Checking in the library or on the Internet is not allowed, and it must be knowledge of event *and* date or nothing! Over the years, as one might imagine, a huge number of events and dates have been offered. Nevertheless, three stand out because they occur again and again. These are the Norman Conquest (1066), the Great Fire of London (1666) and England winning the World Cup (1966). Clearly, the recurrence of the number '6' has something to do with this and once some people start with '1066' they are, self-evidently, very quickly on something of a '66-roll'!

Of these three dates, though, 1066 always occurs the most. It is a date firmly fixed in the popular imagination. More than this, for most people it seems to mark a kind of historical watershed. Before it we find ourselves in a world inhabited by people called Æthelred, Harthacnut and Ælfgifu; afterwards there is a reassuringly familiar world peopled by men and women called William, Henry and Matilda. It is not, therefore, surprising that when, in 1930, W.C. Sellar and R.J. Yeatman wrote their parody of English history they chose to entitle it: *1066 and All That.*

Since this book is so concerned with the events leading up to and causing the trauma of that year it is worth asking some questions. Why is this date so important? Does it justify its place in the popular imagination? Should it really be seen as one of the great milestones of English – and indeed of British – history? As might be expected in any kind of historical debate there is more than one point of view about these questions. Indeed, one might conclude from a general overview of the study of history that to put two historians together will result in the generation of at least three opinions. The study of history is, by its very nature, deeply rooted in debate, argument and controversy. The key events may be relatively easy to fix in time and place (although this should not be taken for granted) but the significance, causation and consequences of events are quite another matter. Here the study of history has argument hard-wired into its character; controversy is endemic. And, for all its iconic status, the events of 1066 are not free from this debate.

An event, the importance of which has been much over-played?

It can be argued that we make too much of the changes brought by the events of 1066 and the Norman Conquest. Much survived these events and provided a lot of the underlying 'landscape' of settlement, taxation and government on which would be played out the events of the next century and well beyond this.

When it came to government, William I, the 'Conqueror' (ruled 1066–87) continued Anglo-Saxon traditions in his newly conquered English realm. He kept the same coronation service, but added 'by hereditary right' and 'grant of God' to the royal titles used; William II (ruled 1087–1100) then added 'by the grace of God' to his official seal. William the Conqueror clearly wanted to present himself as the legitimate inheritor of what had come before. He kept the royal seal in a style comparable to that of Edward the Confessor, but added the king as a knight on one side to remind people of his conquest.

William continued to use the Anglo-Saxon chancery (the official writing office where the Great Seal, used to seal important documents, was kept). No such office had existed in Normandy, but William increased its use and importance; the chancery and royal clerks were very useful in running the country when William was in Normandy. He continued the use of royal writs (official letters giving orders from the king to local areas). These assumed the existence of a strong and centralized government and state, where people in the regions followed royal orders. Again, these had not existed in Normandy and William saw how useful they were. He actually increased their use (first in Old English and later in Latin after 1070).

He kept the well-organized old system of shires, sheriffs (local royal officials), shire courts and hundred (local) courts. At first, Anglo-Saxons remained in post as sheriffs (such as Edric in Wiltshire and Tovi in Somerset), but after 1070 these sheriffs were replaced by Normans. Anglo-Saxon law codes remained in use alongside local juries who gave verdicts under oath on the basis of local knowledge.

Finally, William kept the efficient Anglo-Saxon tax system (the *geld*) and the fines from courts went, as before, to the king, via sheriffs. A system that had milked a prosperous nation and sustained it through decades of Viking Wars now served the new Norman government. The royal Treasury stayed at Winchester. There had been what we would now call 'regime change', but system continuity! Alongside this, William kept the Anglo-Saxon money system, operated at the same mints and by the same moneyers as under his predecessor, Harold II Godwinson; there were similar designs on coins before and after the so-called watershed of 1066. It seems that '1066' had not affected the pound in your pocket (well, the silver pennies, to be precise). It purchased the same pottery and the same food stuff at the same markets.

An event, seared on its century and on the development of the English nation?

But continuity is also about who holds the power *and* a sense of well-being. On both scores there is plenty of evidence to suggest that the Norman Conquest was a political and a cultural earthquake. A large group of 4,500 Anglo-Saxon aristocrats had been replaced by Normans. In 1086 (when *Domesday Book* was compiled) there were 180 – many very wealthy – tenants-in-chief (or *barons*) holding land directly from the king. Of these, only two were Anglo-Saxons. Below these were about 1,400 lesser landowners, of whom only about 100 were Anglo-Saxons. All in all, Anglo-Saxons made up only about 6.5 per cent of landowners.

Under these landowners there were about 6,000 sub-tenants; a substantial number of whom were Anglo-Saxons, but many now leased land that they had owned before Harold Godwinson's defeat in 1066. Their 'feel-good' rating would have been at rock-bottom. Indeed, the *Domesday Book* commissioners at Marsh Gibbon in Buckinghamshire (then just called Marsh) made a rare excursion into human emotions when they recorded how the current landholder, Æthelric, worked the land 'in heaviness and misery'.[1] We can also translate this as: 'miserably and with a heavy heart'.[2] Why was this? It was because, although he had once owned the land in his own right, by 1086 he had been dispossessed and only held it by rent, as the tenant of a Norman lord, William fitzAnsculf. This was what underlay the ending of the world of the 'Æthelrics' and the arrival of the new order of the 'Williams' and their Norman associates.

Some parts of the country faced more than dispossession: they faced annihilation. After a series of northern rebellions against his rule, William took punitive action in the winter of 1069–70, in a merciless destruction of people, livestock, crops, stores and settlements that today is remembered as 'the Harrying of the North'. It led to the death, by starvation, of tens of thousands. A twelfth-century estimate of the death-toll, by the Anglo-Norman chronicler Orderic Vitalis, stood at 100,000. He was aghast at the 'brutal slaughter' of civilians that this involved. He was convinced that such an atrocity 'cannot remain unpunished' by God. Given that, up to this point in his narration of the Norman Conquest, Orderic had largely dutifully followed the determinedly pro-Norman take on events provided by an earlier chronicler, William of Poitiers, this sudden condemnation of William the Conqueror is both shocking and arresting.[3] The chronicler once called Florence of Worcester but now often referred to as John of Worcester, who also wrote in the twelfth century, described the land lying between the rivers Humber and Tees as being devastated. Streams of starving refugees were noted as far south as Evesham in Worcestershire. When *Domesday Book* was compiled, in 1086, somewhere in the region of 60 per cent of land holdings in Yorkshire were described as being 'waste'.

It is possible that the scale of the devastation may have been exaggerated. Orderic Vitalis' mortality figure is probably the result of fairly typical medieval over-estimation. Only one of the 'waste' manors recorded in *Domesday Book* is explicitly attributed to the events of 1069–70.[4] It is further debateable 'whether William had the manpower, time and good weather necessary to reduce vast areas of the region between the Humber and the Tyne to a depopulated, uncultivated desert.'[5] However, even with these qualifications, it is difficult to dismiss entirely the impression given by those writing within a generation of the events, and also the evidence of *Domesday Book*. It is possible, for example, that the 'waste' manors were actually products of 'an administrative or accounting device,'[6] but their location in the right area at the right time looks too significant to be so lightly dismissed; and why was this 'accounting device' not liberally used across the country? No, when all is said and done and the data reviewed and even downgraded, the cumulative evidence that remains is still 'both credible and compelling.'[7] It suggests that something terrible happened in the north.

Culturally, many English people in the generation after the Conquest would have felt like they were living in an occupied land. While its use continued in some areas of literature, it must be recognized that for over two centuries after 1066 the English language went into social decline. Norman-French and Latin (the educated language of the Church) replaced Old English for the elite and the upwardly mobile. William gave up his early attempts to learn English, and England would not have a ruler whose first language was English until Henry IV in 1399. We eat beef, mutton and pork (derived from Norman-French *boef, moton, porc*); but those who care for them in the fields and barns labour with cows, sheep and pigs/swine (derived from Old English *cu, sceap*, Middle English *pigge*/Old English *swin*). The significance of this has been questioned but the implication remains clear: those who worked in the mud and rain spoke English, while those who enjoyed the benefits of their labour spoke Norman-French.

French remained the official language of English government until the 1350s, when the Hundred Years' War with France made its use seem rather unpatriotic. During this period the English that was emerging was different to the Wessex-based Old English of late Anglo-Saxon government and literature. What was emerging was *Middle English.* Therefore, it is no exaggeration to say that the trajectory of the development of the English language was irrevocably changed by 1066; and that is before we take into account the huge number of French words that entered the English vocabulary as a result of the Norman Conquest.

The cultural impact revealed itself in unusual ways. Anglo-Saxon and Danish personal names continued to be given into the twelfth century but then went into a steep decline in favour of new Norman-inspired personal-names such as William, Henry, Geoffrey, Robert, Matilda and Rosamund. In Lincolnshire, in the 1220s, only 6 per cent of tenants in a survey of 624 people had pre-Conquest names, but 14 per cent were called William, 9.5 per cent were called Robert and 6.5 per cent were named John. By 1300, male names were dominated by John, Peter, Thomas and William; female names by Elizabeth, Mary and Anne. The Poll Tax return for Sheffield, in 1379, shows that of the 715 men listed, 33 per cent were named John, 19 per cent were named William. The only Anglo-Saxon name used was Edward and it was not found among the top eight names, which were, in descending order: John, William, Thomas, Richard, Robert, Adam, Henry and Roger.[8] By the thirteenth century we find manorial clerks wearily listing 'another William...' as they unconsciously bore witness to a cultural result of 1066 and the Norman Conquest.

Furthermore, by being part of the Norman and later the Angevin empires, the centre of gravity of English foreign relations was pulled southwards and away from northern Europe and Scandinavia. This significantly altered features of the centre of gravity that had previously existed from 900 to 1066 as a result of the Viking Wars and Scandinavian influence in England during this earlier period of time.

1066 ... a defining date

So, 1066 and the Norman Conquest can easily justify its place in the public consciousness. It was an event of immense importance. It deserves the depth of study it gets and its high profile and, indeed, its iconic status. Anniversaries related to it are justified and fire the imagination. Furthermore, attempting to understand *why* it happened is a crucial part of exploring the national story. Encouraging those outside of the academic world to grapple with this process is well worthwhile because, as well as being dramatic and engaging, 1066 has altered who we are as a nation. 1066 deserves its air-time! And so does the exploration of why it occurred.

But this raises an interesting point, with regard to those causes and our awareness of them, that is both intriguing and puzzling. In thirty-three years of teaching History at secondary level, the year 1066 has always topped the poll when it comes to historic date-popularity. But nobody ever mentioned the 'Viking Conquest of 1016'. Not once. Never...

CHAPTER 2

1016: The 'Forgotten Conquest'

The 'Viking Conquest' of 1016

It is the contention of this book that the 'Viking Conquest' in 1016 led to the much more famous 'Norman Conquest' of 1066. In this sense, the Norman Conquest of 1066 was the culmination of the so-called Viking Wars that had raged across the British Isles for the previous 300 years. These wars were not a continuous conflict. Rather, they were a set of conflicts that had hammered England and its neighbours and which culminated in 1016 in the conquest of England by a Viking king of Denmark, at the head of a mixed Scandinavian army. The victorious Viking king was Cnut and he succeeded in achieving a totality of victory that had eluded previous Viking raiders and invaders. In order to see how this Conquest led to the eventual Norman Conquest, we need to first examine exactly how this 'Viking Conquest' of 1016 occurred. But before we explore the actual events of 1016, it will be helpful to set it in context and to construct a brief résumé of the Viking Wars that led up to this momentous event.[1]

The background to 1016: the Viking Wars, Phase I...

The Viking attacks on Anglo-Saxon England fell into two great phases. The first phase started in the late eighth century. The first recorded attack occurred in 789 when a royal official (the king's reeve) was killed by a group of Vikings at Portland in Dorset; he had ridden down from Dorchester in order to establish the credentials of the visitors and they killed him. The next major event was the much more famous attack on the monastery of Lindisfarne, which occurred in 793; it was an event that sent shock-waves across Western Europe. After this the Viking raids continued to escalate during the ninth century. They were part of a pattern of raids from Scandinavia that targeted the trading settlements either side of the North Sea and the English Channel and which caused severe damage to trade and to the political stability of the kingdoms that were on the receiving end of these raids from the sea.

The push factors behind these raids included: increasing political centralization in Norway and Denmark, as those who lost out in this process looked aboard to further their ambitions; those who had succeeded at home funding their campaigns by raiding abroad; Frankish aggression in turn prompting aggressive defence strategies from Scandinavian communities against their southern neighbours; and changes in the Islamic world disrupted supplies of silver to Scandinavia, so that alternative sources were sought by raiding. All of these combined to encourage expansion outwards, and the inability of those on the receiving end to successfully ward off these attacks meant that raiding soon turned to outright conquest and settlement.

Between 866 and the 890s the raids turned to settlement and obliterated every Anglo-Saxon kingdom with the exception of Alfred the Great's Wessex (the kingdom of the West Saxons). This kingdom alone survived when the Vikings destroyed the other kingdoms of Northumbria, East Anglia and Mercia. In each of these they transformed the political landscape as Viking (mostly Danish) warlords took over the reins of power from the eclipsed Anglo-Saxon royal families. Others, below them in the social scale, became the new local landowners.

The survival of Wessex meant that this Viking conquest was incomplete. By reorganizing his fighting forces, building fortified bases ('*burhs*') and even experimenting in new warship construction, Alfred the Great succeeded in creating a kingdom that was not only able to withstand Viking attacks but was also able, in the reigns of his son and grandson, to conquer the eastern and northern regions of England that had been lost to Danish Viking settlement and political control.

As a result, the Viking attacks declined in the face of the victories of Alfred's son Edward the Elder (ruled 899–924) as he set out to extend the areas under his control. In this he was assisted by his sister, Æthelflæd the 'Lady of the Mercians' and her husband Æthelred, ruler of western Mercia after it became closely allied with Wessex. (Æthelred should not to be confused with the later English king Æthelred II, better known as 'Æthelred *unræd*' or 'Æthelred the unready'.) Together they conquered the East Midlands and East Anglia and brought it under the control of the West Saxons. This combination of West Saxons and Mercians created a newly styled 'Kingdom of the Anglo-Saxons'.

Resurgent Vikings challenged Edward the Elder's son and successor, Athelstan (ruled 924–939); but then met a dramatic defeat at his hands at the battle of Brunanburh in 937. After Athelstan's death, new arrivals of Norse Vikings – originally from Norway but by this time rulers of a Viking kingdom in Dublin – challenged the southern Anglo-Saxon kings for control of the lands north of the river Humber. There the Viking kingdom of York continued as a focus for resistance to the kings from the south. Curiously, perhaps, this resistance combined Scandinavian Vikings with local Northumbrian Anglo-Saxons who preferred a Viking king based in York to a southern Anglo-Saxon king from the traditionally rival kingdom of Wessex! Politics are complicated and there was no simple ethnic divide between Scandinavian Vikings on one side and Anglo-Saxons on the other. This continued until the death of Eric Bloodaxe, the last Viking King of York, in 954.

The Viking Wars Phase II ... why did the Vikings return?

From 954 until 980 it seemed as if all this upheaval was finally a thing of the past. England had become a united kingdom under one ruling dynasty: the one provided by the West Saxons. Indeed, under the rule of King Edgar (ruled 959–75), political stability was finally imposed on this newly united Kingdom of England.

Edgar established an efficient system of coinage and taxation, and this was accompanied by the construction of a naval force that deterred further Viking raiders.[2] It was therefore all the more shocking when, in the reign of Edgar's second son, Æthelred II (ruled 978–1016), the Viking raids resumed. The failure of Æthelred to successfully resist the new wave of raiders led to him later being given the nickname of *unræd*, an Old English word meaning 'no counsel/wisdom' or the 'ill advised'. This was a bitter comment on his actual name since, in Old English, Æthelred meant 'royal counsel/wisdom'. In the twenty-first century he is remembered as 'Æthelred the unready' since the nickname *unræd* sounds like the modern English word 'unready'.[3] It was shortly after the death of Æthelred II in 1016 that the Danish king, Cnut, finally succeeded in conquering England and achieved his 'Viking Conquest'.

Exactly why Phase II of the Viking Wars (which led to conquest in 1016) occurred is a matter of much debate among historians and archaeologists. The exhaustion of the silver mines that had previously supplied the Islamic world appears to have disrupted trade routes between the Middle East and Scandinavia.[4] This caused real problems for Viking-Age communities in Denmark, Sweden and Norway, because they relied on this silver to reward followers and pay tribute to their superiors in the social order.[5] It was to get their hands on this silver that Viking raiding parties seized slaves, in order to turn them into cash when they sold them on to Arab traders or to middlemen who traded with Arabs. At the same time, the growing power of rising states in what is now Russia meant that raiding there for silver was becoming more difficult. All in all there seems to have been a significant decline in the eastern trade routes, and this undoubtedly explains why Swedish Vikings eventually joined in the new phase of Viking attacks on England. (Before this, the raids on the British Isles had been undertaken by Danes and Norwegians.)

By a coincidence (happy for silver-poor Vikings and unhappy for newly silver-rich Western Europeans) the discovery of new silver sources in the Harz Mountains in the 960s meant that Western Europe was now experiencing an abundance of silver, which was used in coins and ornaments. For Vikings intent on replenishing their stocks of silver this provided an immense opportunity, both by stealing large amounts of silver and by threatening extreme violence unless they were bought off. This is why huge quantities of English silver pennies turn up on archaeological sites in Scandinavia: somewhere in the region of 37,920,000 individual silver pennies were shipped across the North Sea, and finds of English silver pennies in hoards from Scandinavia increase massively in the period 978–1035. About 35,000 such coins have been discovered in Scandinavia to date.[6] They are testament to the extortion of vast amounts of wealth from England during this period.

This policy of extortion was further stimulated by the emergence of more unified Viking-Age kingdoms in Denmark and in Norway. This gave rulers there greater resources with which to fund military adventures abroad, and since their tax-raising systems were nowhere near as developed as those of Anglo-Saxon England, the deficit could be rectified by raiding England.

In Denmark a more unified state emerged in the early tenth century. This was under King Gorm and later, in the 960s, this trend was accelerated when Harald Bluetooth extended Danish rule into Norway. This increase in Danish royal authority led to the construction of a massive military barracks-complex at Trelleborg on Zealand, where a circular fortress (probably dating from around 980) was constructed. This was just one of four similar complexes. Their construction probably dates from late in the reign of Harald Bluetooth and they probably protected his royal authority from both internal and external threats. Denmark was becoming a serious military power as its royal authority became better able to unite and utilize resources. At the same time, Harald became a Christian and was responsible for the conversion of the Danes. The unifying nature of Harald Bluetooth's reign inspired the Swedish IT company Ericsson to call its open-wireless technology 'Bluetooth' since, like Harald, it unites and utilizes otherwise scattered resources.

However, it was not only Denmark that was experiencing greater unification. In Norway too, after a decisive naval battle at Hafrsfjord in 872, Harald Finehair came to dominate a generally more united Norwegian kingdom. His power tailed off the further north he went, but his achievement helps explain the increased presence of Norwegian Vikings – alongside Danish ones – in the armies that descended on England in Phase II of the Viking Wars. They would not, however, be as influential as Danes, since Harald Finehair's unification was built on less secure foundations than had been achieved in Denmark. On his death, Norwegian unity fractured and Danish kings were quick to take advantage of this and interfere in Norwegian affairs, often ruling areas of Norway through subservient local earls.

This period of weakness was reversed in the late tenth century when a Norwegian, Olaf Tryggvason (died c.1000), briefly managed to occupy the Norwegian throne independently of Denmark. He, too, was active in raiding England, as we shall shortly see. When he died this Norwegian independence was threatened and after the death of his successor, Olaf Haraldsson (St Olav) in 1030, the Danish king, Cnut, re-established Danish control over Norway for a time. However, Norway was restless under Danish rule and when Cnut died, in 1035, Olaf Haraldsson's son, Magnus the Good, took back the Norwegian throne. He himself was succeeded by a tough warrior-king named Harald Hardrada, who invaded England at a critical point in 1066 and then was killed at the battle of Stamford Bridge on 25 September 1066.

This is getting ahead of our story, but it shows just how significant Scandinavians were in the history of England in the period running up to 1066 and in the events of that momentous year. But to return to the events leading up to 1016, what is clear is that a recently unified Denmark and a more unified Norway posed a massive threat to England. A great storm was gathering in Scandinavia and it was soon to break on England with dramatic results. And, as this 'storm' broke, it would be two Viking rulers who would play a major part in the events leading to the 'Viking Conquest' of 1016. These two rulers were Olaf Tryggvason of Norway and Svein Forkbeard of Denmark.

The first of these, Olaf Tryggvason, ruled Norway from 995 to c.1000. The grandson of Harald Finehair, he came from a Norwegian royal family that had an interest in – and a knowledge of – England. Earlier members of the family included Eric Bloodaxe, who had been King of York until 954. Like Harald Bluetooth in Denmark, Olaf Tryggvason played an active role in promoting the Christian conversion of Norway. However, we know frustratingly little about him due to the late arrival of literacy in Scandinavia. From the English side he appears in a few short references in the *Anglo-Saxon Chronicle*. From the continent the only other near-contemporary account is Adam of Bremen's *Gesta Hammaburgensis Ecclesiae Pontificum* (*Deeds of the Archbishops of Hamburg*), which was written in about 1070. In the late twelfth century he also featured in two Icelandic sagas.[7] These, though, are very late sources and it is clear that by the time they were written history and legend were firmly intertwined. A similarly late source was compiled by an Icelandic writer named Snorri Sturluson, in his *Heimskringla* (*Circle of the World*). This was intended as a history of Norway from prehistoric times to 1177 and was written in about 1230.

According to the later sagas, Olaf Tryggvason gained early military experience in the Baltic, raiding the neighbouring tribes of the Slavs and Balts on the southern and eastern shores of the Baltic. Situated on the trade routes between the Middle East and Scandinavia, they offered rich pickings to Viking raiders. It was after this that Olaf Tryggvason, now an experienced warrior and leader, turned his attention to England. The Anglo-Saxon sources first record him as raiding Folkestone in Kent in 991, with a fleet of ninety-three ships. He was bought off with £10,000. This was a pointer to things to come: soon vast amounts of Anglo-Saxon silver would be flowing to Scandinavia to buy off Viking armies.

However, Olaf Tryggvason was not alone in his lucrative targeting of England. At the same time, Svein Forkbeard, King of Denmark, began launching raids too. Named from his distinctive facial hair, Svein Forkbeard ruled Denmark between 985 and 1014. As well as this, he briefly ruled England for five short weeks before dying in 1014. This was a prelude to the successful conquest achieved by his son, Cnut, two years later, in 1016. Svein Forkbeard appears in the *Anglo-Saxon Chronicle*, but in a greater number of annals than does Olaf Tryggvason. His exploits were also recorded by Adam of Bremen and in *Heimskringla*. These, though, are not the only written verdicts on him: in addition to these sources, he also features in a document called the *Encomium Emmae Reginae* (*In Praise of Queen Emma*), which is an eleventh-century account (written c.1040–42), composed in honour of Emma, Cnut's queen. We will hear a lot more about this document and about the Norman princess and English queen, Emma, and her marriages to both Æthelred II, 'the unready', *and* his Viking nemesis, Cnut, for she plays an important part in the interweaving of events that linked England, Normandy and Scandinavia in the early eleventh century.

According to a later Icelandic saga – the thirteenth-century *Jómsvíkinga saga* (*Saga of the Jómsvíkings*) – Svein Forkbeard was raised among the *Jómsvíkings*, a semi-legendary group of Viking mercenaries. Whether this is true is impossible to say, since this source (as with so many Icelandic sagas) intermingles history and legend in a manner now difficult, if not impossible, to disentangle.

What we do know, though, is that Svein Forkbeard was the son of the Harald Bluetooth who we met earlier – the king who had first unified Denmark. The family story was not a happy one, since Svein Forkbeard only became king after he had deposed his father in 985. This was the period in which he also began his raids on England: clearly, he now had the combination of ambition and resources to launch attacks on the wealthy state across the North Sea. In 994, he joined Olaf Tryggvason in a campaign of attacks on England. In the near future, tensions would develop between these two rulers over influence in Norway (an old bone of contention), but in the early 990s they had a project that benefited them both and which drew them together in an effective alliance: attacking England.

In this they were helped by a combination of a young king and dynastic instability in England: Æthelred II was only in his early teens, and some believed him to be implicated in the murder of the previous king, his half-brother, Edward King and Martyr. Vikings were adept at exploiting any sign of political division and would punish England for this in increasing measure in the years running up to 1016. The Latin version of the *Anglo-Saxon Chronicle* that is found in the bilingual so-called manuscript F (compiled c.1100–1109) alleges that the problems of England in Phase II of the Viking Wars had started with the troubled accession of Æthelred II and continued from there on. England was about to pay a very high price in blood and treasure for lack of political unity.

The storm breaks on England...

We have a very detailed account of the crisis that engulfed England during the reign of Æthelred II and this is found in a source already referred to: the *Anglo-Saxon Chronicle*. This vitally important document was first compiled in the late ninth century and recounted the history of Anglo-Saxon England (and especially Wessex) up to that point. To do so it drew on a wide range of sources and traditions, many of which are otherwise unknown to us today, although it also drew on other sources that have survived, which gives us an opportunity to compare viewpoints. This original version of the *Chronicle* no longer exists but historians refer to it as 'the common stock'; it was distributed to a number of key monasteries, which added information to it reflecting their own viewpoints and continued to do so in the following couple of centuries. The longest continuation of the *Chronicle* was at Peterborough, where the monks continued to add to it until as late as 1154.

These different manuscripts of the *Chronicle* often offer us different viewpoints on events and are an interesting barometer of the opinions associated with particular regions and factions within late Anglo-Saxon England. Some tenth- and eleventh-century events were recorded very close to the time of the action being described. In these cases we are reading something approaching contemporary opinion. But it is *opinion* and we should not forget that. At other times (as we shall shortly see) sections of annals were written after what we now call regime-change, and in these cases we are dealing with interpretations that give a particular verdict on what were then current events and those of a discredited recent past; what we might now call political spin! This is not to dismiss the *Chronicle*, because it is a vital source of information. It is merely to remind us that – as with all historical sources of evidence – we need to recognize *interpretation* as well as *record* in the accounts that these annals leave us. History is all the more interesting and challenging for this, so this should not be read as an apology. But it can be a challenge.

From the *Chronicle* we can see how Viking attacks escalated from the 980s. In 981 the south-west of England suffered and we hear how

St Petroc's monastery at Padstow in Cornwall was sacked by raiders. In 982 the attacks shifted eastward when Portland in Dorset – the location of the very first Viking raid in 789 – experienced a heavy raid and, that same year, London was attacked and burned; as a major commercial centre it offered rich rewards for raiding forces in both material and slaves. This was then followed by a brief pause in attacks, but it did not last. In 988 Watchet in Somerset was devastated.

Who was carrying out these raids? We have already examined the threat posed by Vikings from Denmark and Norway, but the situation in this early period was more complex and more fluid. Reflection on the geographical spread of these raids (with the exception of that on London) suggests that they were conducted by Irish Sea Vikings. Based in Ireland and using temporary bases such as the island of Flatholm (the Norse word for 'fleet island') in the Bristol Channel, they were free to raid into Wales and England. There is hard evidence to support this interpretation, since archaeologists have noted that Anglo-Saxon coin dies – used in the mints at Bath, Watchet and Lydford – were later used to strike Viking coins in Dublin from about 995 onwards.[8] Clearly, these useful tools in coin production had been seized in raids, since it is difficult to imagine any other way by which such products of the excellent and highly centralized Anglo-Saxon coinage system could have got into enemy hands.

If the early raids were planned in Ireland, it is clear that what was to follow had its origins in Norway and Denmark. Raids changed in intensity in 991 and it is clear that they had moved up a gear. That year witnessed the first great campaign of Olaf Tryggvason on Folkestone and Sandwich. After these attacks the raiders moved north and eventually landed at Maldon in Essex. It was there that the ealdorman (the king's regional representative) of Essex, named Byrhtnoth, controversially allowed a Viking army to cross the causeway in order to fight them and then lost the battle that followed, in heroic style. As one French observer commented on the Charge of the Light Brigade of 1854, '*C'est magnifique, mais ce n'est pas la guerre*' ('It is magnificent, but it is not war'). One might be tempted to say the same about Byrhtnoth's heroic gesture in allowing the Vikings to cross the causeway in order to line up for a decisive battle, as opposed to making them face the Anglo-Saxon forces that were successfully blocking their approach.

A poem – *The Battle of Maldon* – offers us heroic ambiguity in how it describes the battle's outcome. Line 89 states that Byrhtnoth's decision was driven '*for his ofermode*'. In other words, it was due to either his 'confidence' or his 'pride'. The Old English word *ofermode* can convey both senses and so we do not know if the poet thought the decision was an honourable gamble (to prevent the raiders causing chaos elsewhere) or an act of pride that led to disaster. This is not helped by the fact that we are not entirely sure when the poem was written. It may have been a near-contemporary record written at the monastery of Ely where Byrhtnoth was buried, in which case the positive spin is the most likely: Byrhtnoth failed but his heroic death should inspire other acts of heroic resistance to Viking depredations. Alternatively, it may have been composed after the Viking Conquest of 1016 as a defiant defence of Anglo-Saxon virtues and a rejection of the Viking Danish rule of Cnut: we lost but the moral victory of our heroism outweighs Viking success. Then again it may have been written after the re-establishment of Anglo-Saxon rule in 1042, in which case the moral is: we won in the end. Finally, some think it was written after the Norman Conquest of 1066 in which case the message was: Anglo-Saxons fought bravely but the descendants of Vikings finally won. If the latter, it would be a neat reminder of the message of this book: the Vikings caused the Norman Conquest!

Weighing up all the options, it is likely that it was a near-contemporary composition and written before the implications of such heroic failure were apparent (the Vikings were going to eventually win).[9] The contrast between heroic defiance and failure in the poem is profound. As one who studied the memorable poem once commented, 'Byrhtnoth himself is remembered in this poem as a wordsmith rather than a warsmith.'[10] Whatever we eventually conclude regarding the decision made by Byrhtnoth, we are left with a picture of Anglo-Saxon warriors laying down their lives around the body of their fallen leader in brave self-sacrifice.[11] As one old warrior, faced with impending death, puts it in the poem, 'Thoughts must be the braver, heart more valiant, courage the greater as our strength grows less.'[12] This is stirring stuff, even if *'ce n'est pas la guerre'*.

The same year that Byrhtnoth and his companions were dying at Maldon, the Anglo-Saxon state made a huge payment of £10,000 to persuade the Viking army to leave. For Olaf Tryggvason it had been a very profitable summer; it was the bloody start of a Viking business enterprise that would eventually drain tens of thousands of pounds of silver out of the English economy. And the raids were only just starting!

Winston Churchill said of Dunkirk, 'We must be very careful not to assign to this the attributes of a victory. Wars are not won by evacuations.' Æthelred II might have had his own verdict on events such as the Battle of Maldon: wars are not won by heroic defeats. Wars are won by victories and these were made more difficult to achieve by political treachery. It is hard now to disentangle all the complicated strands of political ambition, rivalry and treason that motivated some members of the Anglo-Saxon elite at this crucial period of history: the *Chronicle* is adamant that there was a lack of loyalty and determination in some quarters, and even if we conclude that some of this was later special-pleading in order to excuse earlier failures, it is difficult to dismiss it all. In 992 the Ealdorman of Hampshire, Ælfric, was accused of warning a Viking army that, as a result of his actions, escaped an Anglo-Saxon ambush. The same Viking force then went on to inflict a defeat on the Anglo-Saxon naval force sent to intercept it.

In 993 another act of treason is recorded. In this year an English army facing Vikings who had landed in the Humber estuary was betrayed by its own three leaders: they fled from the battle and resistance collapsed. What was going on? A later chronicler accused those who fled in this instance of being descended from earlier Danish settlers. The implication of this was clear: Danes already settled in England since the ninth century could not be trusted. When push came to shove, they would cheer for Denmark not England. This may have been true or it may have been that those in an ethnic minority were useful scapegoats for Anglo-Saxon and later chroniclers who were looking for someone to blame for the disaster. As we shall soon see, this search for scapegoats could be driven by those at the highest level of Anglo-Saxon government. What is definite in 992 is that Æthelred II was furious at the failure/treachery of Ealdorman Ælfric, since he punished his son by the horrific sentence of blinding (a sentence that will feature in another and more famous incident later in this story).

In the year 994 the first recorded joint attack by Olaf Tryggvason of Norway and Svein Forkbeard of Denmark occurred, when their joint army unsuccessfully attacked London. They did, however, cause immense damage and, worse, they then over-wintered in Southampton. As well as being a disaster for this town, it meant that the campaigning season of 995 could start all the earlier. The danger was all too clear to the Anglo-Saxon leadership and that winter some high-level and secret negotiations took place. We would like to know more about these but we cannot now discover what occurred. However, we can be sure that they did happen because, in the spring, something momentous took place: Olaf Tryggvason took part in a Christian Confirmation ceremony at Andover with Æthelred II as his sponsor; it is likely that Olaf had been baptised elsewhere and this ceremony confirmed his new faith and an alliance with Æthelred II. As part of this, Olaf promised to end his attacks. We can only imagine what Svein Forkbeard said about this strategy, which had split his alliance with the Norwegians! However, in about the year 1000 Olaf died and the initiative passed to Svein.

If the clever negotiations of the winter of 994–5 had seemed to offer a counter-strategy to the Viking skill at exploiting divisions among enemies, the success was not to last. What was worse, the Anglo-Saxon elites appeared to offer many opportunities for Viking raiders seeking to make the most of a lack of resolute resistance. Devon was devastated in 997; in 998, Dorset suffered similarly. The *Chronicle* bitterly comments:

'as soon as they [the English forces] were to have joined battle, a flight was always instigated by some means, and always the enemy had the victory in the end.'[13] The *Chronicle* entries for 999 and 1001 contain similar references to betrayal and failure. Another huge payment, of £24,000, was made in 1002 to buy off the attackers. When assessing these annals we need to bear in mind that modern research has demonstrated that they were written after the final Viking victory in 1016. As such, they viewed past events through the lens of that event, which made it seem that defeat had been inevitable. But things were bad enough and at the highest level of Anglo-Saxon government plans began to be discussed to bring retribution down on the heads of the foreigners held responsible for these humiliations.

The Massacre of St Brice's Day, 1002

The *Chronicle* records an event that occurred on 13 November 1002 and, today, is commonly known as 'The Massacre of St Brice's Day'. On this day, the *Chronicle* says that 'the king ordered to be slain all the Danish men who were in England – this was done on St Brice's day – because the king had been informed that they would treacherously deprive him, and then all his councillors, of life, and possess this kingdom afterwards'.[14] This act appears to have been sanctioned at the highest level of the Anglo-Saxon state and it impacted on Scandinavians who were themselves at the top of their own social order. Writing in the twelfth century, the chronicler William of Malmesbury claimed that those killed included Svein Forkbeard's sister, along with her husband, Pallig, and their child. This was, apparently, in response to an earlier act of betrayal by Pallig since the *Chronicle* claims that, in the previous year, he had betrayed Æthelred II. This suggests that, like Olaf Tryggvason, he had entered into an alliance with the English king and had thus been (temporarily if the *Chronicle* is correct) drawn away from allegiance to Svein Forkbeard.

Given the apparently widespread nature of the massacre, it has left little corroboratory evidence in other sources. One that does survive, though, is a replacement document issued by Æthelred II to St Frideswide's church in Oxford. The issuing of a replacement was necessary because the church's original document had been destroyed when the church was burned during the massacre of the Danes – it was to this building that Danes living in Oxford had retreated in 1002, and the pursuing townspeople had set fire to the building and burned them to death. The document in question dates from 7 December 1004, and famously describes how 'all the Danes who had sprung up in this island, sprouting like cockle [a weed] amongst the wheat, were to be destroyed by a most just extermination.'[15]

The record of the *Chronicle*, combined with that for St Frideswide's, leaves us with the impression of a national destruction of Danes who had settled in England. In fact, this could not have happened since Danish settlers had settled in eastern England since the ninth century and were well integrated into English society. Indeed, in large parts of the east and north of England there was really an Anglo-Danish society. Æthelred II simply did not have the resources to massacre all the Danes living in England – even had he so wished. The *Chronicle* must be over-stating the case. Many of those who were killed were, in all probability, Danish merchants whose activities linked communities living either side of the North Sea. If they had settled in England since the start of Phase II of the Viking Wars they would probably have been easily identified by language and dress and, therefore, more easily targeted. It is also possible that those killed were actually Viking mercenaries who had changed sides and sworn allegiance to Æthelred II (such as Olaf Tryggvason and Pallig) but whose allegiance was suspect.[16]

Furthermore, it is possible (indeed likely) that the massacre was confined to a handful of prominent towns, such as Oxford, whatever the claims made in the *Chronicle*. This would have been more likely if these newcomers constituted a recognizable social group that stood out from their Anglo-Saxon neighbours. Oxford may have featured in the massacre in a disproportionate manner as it is in Oxford that a significant execution cemetery, containing the bodies of thirty-seven people, has been excavated. Most of those examined were males, aged between sixteen and twenty-five when they died: this suggests men of military-age. In addition, a study of their bones indicates that they had eaten a great deal of seafood during their lives. Given the distance of Oxford from the coast, this indicates young men involved in some kind of maritime occupation. It is very likely that they were Scandinavian mercenaries killed in 1002.[17]

Whatever the exact focus of the Massacre of St Brice's Day, there is also other evidence to show that things did not always go the way that Viking raiders intended. In three months of excavation, in 2009, archaeologists working on the South Dorset Ridgeway some four miles north of Weymouth found fifty-four headless bodies and fifty-one skulls. The bodies had been deposited – in one episode of killing – in a silted-up and disused quarry pit dating from the Roman period. The fact that the skulls were piled together on the southern edge of the pit made it obvious that those buried had all been decapitated. The total absence of belt buckles or brooches indicates that they had been naked at the time of death. The position of the skeletons revealed that their hands had not been bound; perhaps indicating a degree of courage and self-control among those killed. All were male. Most were aged between eighteen and twenty-five (a very similar age-range to the bodies excavated at Oxford), with the youngest in their early teens and the oldest over fifty years of age. Most, though not all, had a physique in keeping with warrior status.

Radiocarbon dating revealed that they had died in the period 970–1025. Analysis of strontium and oxygen isotopes in the teeth and of the collagen from the bones indicated that they grew up in various places within Scandinavia, that they had lived there in later life, that they had mixed 'migratory histories', and that they had mixed diets. In short, they were by origin Scandinavian but were not a uniform group. Nevertheless, they had all died together in one episode that was clearly an execution. Curiously, none of the bones indicated previous battle-wounds and some of the individuals were in poor health. This has led some to question whether they were a Viking raiding party (the obvious conclusion from the other evidence).

The execution was messy: heads had been removed only as a result of several attempts from a variety of angles. Some blows had struck the top of the head and others the shoulder blades; on average, each individual received almost four wounds. Cuts to hands, arms and the top and side of heads may indicate defensive reactions by those killed but, if so, do not constitute significant resistance. This indicates an organized event but one that soon disintegrated into fairly chaotic violence.[18] On balance, it is probably best to conclude that those executed were the crews of captured Viking raiding ships. Some of the anomalies (such as the health of individuals) may simply be reminders that a Viking raiding party constituted a mixed bunch, not an elite group of super-fit warriors, as such groups may have attracted males from a wide range of backgrounds and with a varied degree of physical fitness.

In 1002 Æthelred II's strategies extended beyond vengeance. In a policy designed to encourage 'poachers' to act as 'gamekeepers', he married Emma of Normandy. She was from the ruling class of settlers, descended from Vikings, that had gained control of this part of France. It was clearly part of an alliance designed to prevent new Viking armies from using Normandy as a base from which to launch attacks on England. It was an astute move, but one with unforeseen consequences. Unknown to Æthelred II it was the beginning of a Norman connection that, sixty-four years later, would lead to the Norman Conquest of 1066 and the destruction of the Anglo-Saxon state. But in 1002 all that lay in the future and before that Norman Conquest occurred, a Viking Conquest would intervene.

The return of Svein Forkbeard

The Viking attacks were not all under the command of famous leaders. Indeed, in a number of cases we do not know who was in overall command. This changed in 1003 when the *Chronicle* again refers to Svein Forkbeard by name, his first named appearance since 994. In that year, Exeter was captured by Svein. As on previous occasions this was due to treachery on the part of a member of the Anglo-Saxon elite. Later on in that year's campaign the ealdorman Ælfric was alleged to have shirked his duty by pretending to be suffering from sickness 'and began retching to vomit'.[19] The episode of vomiting meant he did not attack. This was the same Ælfric whose son had been blinded in 992, so why he had been allowed to remain in his post is something of a mystery. He was one of a number of elite Anglo-Saxons whose loyalty was in question but who were not removed from office; either they were too powerful to challenge or this indicates a shocking lack of competence on the part of the government of Æthelred II.

In 1003 Svein sacked Norwich and Thetford, then in 1005 a great famine struck England; the later chronicler, John of Worcester, claimed that Svein returned to Denmark as a result of this famine. Viking forces returned in 1006, since the *Chronicle* for 1006 refers to so much damage that 'they [the Viking army] had cruelly left their mark on every shire of Wessex with their burning and their harrying.'[20] As a result, a massive payment of £36,000 was made in order to buy them off.

Resistance crumbles

From 1006 onwards English resistance went into steep decline.[21] At first this was not obvious. Æthelred II ordered an expansion of the navy in order to intercept Viking raiders at sea; this strategy failed because, in 1009, the all-too-predictable internal disputes led to a section of the fleet rebelling. The mutinous ships were under the control of Wulfnoth Cild of Sussex, a south coast landowner who will feature again in this story because he was probably the father of Earl Godwin, whose son would take the throne in 1066 as Harold II Godwinson.

The episode with Wulfnoth Cild of Sussex casts light on the internal rivalries that were dividing the Anglo-Saxon elite at this time, something that Æthelred II failed to resolve. It seems that another nobleman named Beorhtric charged Wulfnoth before the king with accusations that do not appear in the surviving records. It may have been a justifiable charge or an attempt to undermine a rival. The later chronicler, John of Worcester, records a tradition that the accusations were baseless; this is possible since, as we shall see, Beorhtric's brother, Eadric Streona, was soon deeply implicated in treachery that undermined Anglo-Saxon resistance and also led to the deaths of rivals within the Anglo-Saxon upper class. In 1009, though, Wulfnoth Cild was clearly not trusting royal justice to save him. Instead, he deserted the fleet, taking with him twenty ships, and proceeded to attack the south coast.

This strange practice of attacking one's own countrymen occurred on a number of occasions. Harold II Godwinson's sons did so in the West Country after their father was killed at Hastings, and this was by no means an isolated occurrence. It may have been motivated by a desire to strike at the economic resources of rivals, or simply a desire to cause such a nuisance that charges against the leader involved would be dropped. Whichever was the motivation, those civilians whose loved ones were killed and homes burned must have had bitter words to describe such pursuit of politics by other methods. In 1009, Beorhtric followed Wulf-noth Cild with eighty ships, but a storm drove his fleet ashore and it was burned by Wulfnoth. It was a very unhappy ending to an episode designed to improve Anglo-Saxon naval capabilities.

As if things were not bad enough, a huge Danish army landed that summer under the leadership of a Viking named Thorkell the Tall; the first appearance of this particular Viking leader. Once again Anglo-Saxon defences were undermined by treachery. According to the *Chronicle* the man responsible for hampering the English resistance was Eadric Streona – brother of the Beorhtric who had earlier precipitated the crisis involving Wulfnoth Cild. Eadric Streona had been the Ealdorman of Mercia since 1007 and his career was on an upward trajectory since he was to become the dominant member of the Anglo-Saxon aristocracy by 1012.[22] With such lack of determination at the top of the Anglo-Saxon hierarchy, things could only deteriorate further. In 1010, Thorkell's army caused immense damage in East Anglia, Oxfordshire and Buckingham-shire. Reflecting on the events of that year the compiler of the *Chronicle* lamented, 'When they were in the east, the English army was kept in the west, and when they were in the south, our army was in the north, and no policy was followed-through and each shire looked to its own defence.'[23]

Without a united strategy and resolution the Anglo-Saxon state seemed doomed. Why did members of the Anglo-Saxon elite appear so irresolute or disloyal? The answer may be that, looking at these events from a twenty-first century perspective, we are expecting too much in terms of a united patriotic response. At the time it seems that members of the elite may have given up on the future of Æthelred II's govern-ment. This, combined with a sense of family and regional loyalties (rather than 'national' loyalty), may have persuaded them that their interests lay in accommodating the invaders.[24] This is possible but each had sworn loyalty to their king and so, even given these possibly mitigating circum-stances, we are still left with betrayal.

In 1011 the Viking army captured Canterbury and took Archbishop Ælfheah hostage; what happened next horrified contemporaries. The German chronicler, Thietmar of Merseburg, recorded a tradition that Ælfheah attempted to raise his own ransom but failed. Following this,

Thorkell the Tall offered to pay it himself, but Ælfheah would not allow anyone else to ransom him. The slightly later account in the *Chronicle* also indicates that he refused to have a ransom paid to buy him out of Viking custody. In all probability he knew the high level of taxation that was being extorted out of his fellow-countrymen in order to pay-off Viking armies and refused to add to their tax-burden. The twelfth-century chronicler, John of Worcester, recorded a tradition that the Vikings upped their demands and called for an additional payment of £3,000 for the archbishop's life, and that it was this that led to his refusal to cooperate. Whatever the truth, it is clear that violent extortion was hard-wired into the Viking strategies.

In 1012, despite receiving a payment of £48,000, the Vikings murdered the archbishop. In a drunken state they hurled ox-bones and ox-skulls at him, which culminated in striking him on the head with the back of an axe. He died. The *Chronicle* summed up the context to this murder: the Vikings were 'greatly incensed against the bishop because he would not promise them any money, but forbade that anything should be paid for him. They were also very drunk, for wine from the south had been brought there.'[25] Even hardened Vikings were shocked at this drunken violence and Thorkell the Tall, who had offered to ransom the archbishop, deserted to the English. Paying for Thorkell's army was now added to the English tax bill: in one way or another, Vikings were draining England of silver.

Corroborative evidence points to the huge scale of this smash-and-grab strategy. In Uppland, in Sweden, a runic memorial stone records that: 'Áli had this stone put up in his own honour. He took Knútr's [Cnut's] *danegeld* in England.'[26] This may refer to a later payment since, technically, the term *Danegeld* (Dane-tax) was not recorded until after the Norman Conquest, when it was used to describe recurring taxes paid to the crown. Before this the random massive payments of tribute (*gafol*) were not formalized until 1012, when an annual levy based on land ownership was introduced to pay for the army of Thorkell the Tall. This was the *heregeld* (army-tax), and it continued to be collected until 1051, when it was temporarily suspended by Edward the Confessor. It was later reinstated, possibly as early as 1052, and it was then collected annually until 1066.

Something very much like the *heregeld* was levied after the Norman Conquest in 1066, and it was then termed '*Danegeld*' as an indicator of its origins in the annual tax started in 1012. It continued to be collected until 1161, when the last *Danegeld* was collected by Henry II, long after the end of the Viking Wars. So, to be precise, the irregular payments to Viking raiders, after 991, should be described as *gafol* (tribute); the annual taxation to pay for Scandinavian mercenary units (between 1012 and 1051) as *heregeld* or *geld*; and the term *Danegeld* reserved for the later resumption of this system of taxes. However, *Danegeld* is also frequently used today to describe the general collection of money to pay off Danish invaders and, as such, it has passed into common usage.[27]

The stone from Uppland reveals that Swedish Vikings were now operating in the army of Cnut of Denmark. Another rune-stone, which is also from Uppland, records that another Viking, named Ulf, 'took three payments of *geld* in England. The first was the one that Tosti paid, then Thorkell, then Cnut'.[28] Tosti was a Swedish Viking, whose daughter married Svein Forkbeard.

While the actual figures quoted by the *Chronicle* may be questioned, the scale of the extraction of money from England is beyond dispute. The figures are staggering: between 991 and 1012 they add up to £137,000. In 1014 Thorkell the Tall and his men were paid £21,000. In 1018 Cnut (ruler of England since 1016) took a massive further payment of £82,500. This comes to a total of £240,500 and does not take account of the (unknown) sum from the *heregeld* that was siphoned off after 1016 to pay for Cnut's mercenaries following his taking of the throne.[29] In short, the equivalent in today's money of billions of pounds was pulled out of the English economy by Viking demands. It should be noted, by way of scale, that a fully grown pig cost 6 pence (with 240 pennies in each £1) and that the combined value of all the estates of Glastonbury – the wealthiest abbey in 1066 – was in the region of £820.

The 'Viking Conquest', 1016

In the year 1013, Svein Forkbeard of Denmark returned to England at the head of a Viking army with the goal of conquest. He swiftly secured the submission of the Northumbrians, parts of Lincolnshire and other areas of the eastern Midlands; this was followed by the submission of Oxford, Winchester and Bath. At Bath the landowners of the West Country accepted his rule. Resistance was melting away. After over twenty years of warfare, England was exhausted. The only exception was London. Æthelred II was there in person and, for now, it held firm. However, as the scale of collapse became apparent he bowed to the inevitable and fled to his wife's family in Normandy; it was ironic that he sought shelter with the descendants of Vikings. Svein Forkbeard of Denmark was King of England and an Anglo-Danish empire. But this first Viking Conquest was a false start, for on 3 February 1014 he died. He was succeeded by Cnut, his son.

It was then that the frailty of the allegiance of the Anglo-Saxon elites revealed itself. It was clear that they had only submitted earlier out of necessity, for with Svein dead they sent messengers to Normandy and recalled Æthelred II; Cnut had no choice but to abandon his newly

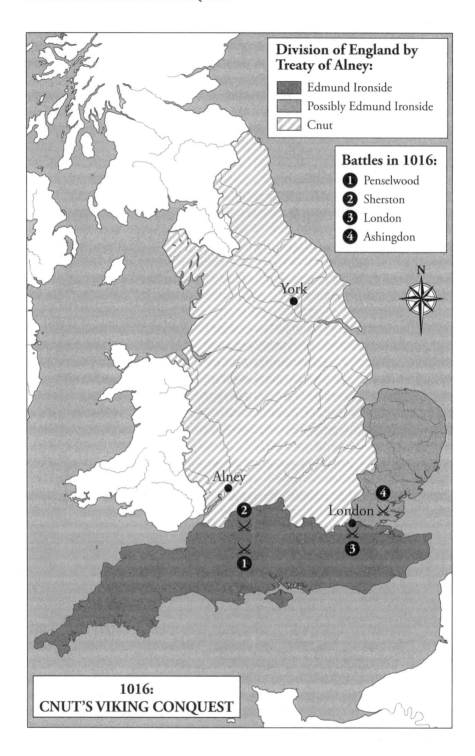

Division of England by Treaty of Alney:
- Edmund Ironside
- Possibly Edmund Ironside
- Cnut

Battles in 1016:
1. Penselwood
2. Sherston
3. London
4. Ashingdon

N

York

Alney

London

1016:
CNUT'S VIKING CONQUEST

acquired kingdom. But before he left he mutilated those given to him as hostages and put these crippled individuals ashore at Sandwich (Kent). Then he sailed for Denmark.

The year 1015 did not start well for Anglo-Saxon political stability. The royal court was divided between a faction loyal to Eadric Streona and a faction loyal to the ætheling (royal prince) Edmund Ironside (a son of Æthelred II from an earlier marriage). For reasons that are difficult to fathom Æthelred II backed Eadric Streona, in spite of his treasonable track-record. And treason was accompanied by murder, for during a meeting of the royal council held at Oxford, Eadric Streona had key rivals murdered. This seems to have occurred with the agreement of Æthelred II, whose lack of political judgement was staggering. Faced with this alliance of Eadric Streona with his own father, Edmund Ironside cut loose. He married the widow of one of the men murdered at Oxford and rallied the eastern Midlands in support of his cause. Then Cnut returned. A rune-stone from Galteland, Norway reads, concerning a man named Biórr: 'He was killed in the guard when Knútr [Cnut] attacked England.'[30] Clearly, there were Norwegians as well as Danes and Swedes in Cnut's army.

Things rapidly began to unravel from an Anglo-Saxon perspective. Dorset, Wiltshire and Somerset were devastated. Æthelred II was too ill to lead his army and Edmund Ironside was betrayed by Eadric Streona, who went over to Cnut. Eadric Streona was nothing if not consistent! Clearly, the only driving force for him was his own personal ambition and now that seemed best served by recognizing the inevitable: the victory of Cnut. Another key player – Ealdorman Uhtred of Northumbria – also submitted to Cnut. He was promptly murdered, and one manuscript of the *Chronicle* claims it was on the advice of Eadric Streona.

In April, Æthelred II died. Edmund succeeded to the kingdom but immediately had to fight battles at Penselwood (Somerset) and Sherston (Wiltshire). In the latter he was once more betrayed by Eadric Streona, who had switched sides and then switched again. Edmund was eventually reconciled to Eadric Streona, who then betrayed the king yet again at the bitterly contested battle of Ashingdon in Essex. With neither side able to break the stalemate, Edmund and Cnut met at Alney in Gloucestershire and agreed to divide England: Cnut took Mercia and Edmund took Wessex. Before the year was out, Edmund Ironside was dead, cause unknown, Cnut took the kingdom. He was king of Denmark and of England, and would rule the two nations until his death in 1035.

It was 1016, the year of the Viking Conquest. Its consequences would dictate many of the events that followed in the next fifty years. It was a complex conquest that had muddled the differences between Anglo-Saxons and Scandinavians. Æthelred II had, at various times, secured the support of Viking chieftains such as Pallig and Thorkell the Tall. Edmund Ironside had opposed Cnut with an army raised in the Danish areas of eastern England (the 'Danelaw'). This reveals his ability to inspire confidence in areas that might otherwise have been expected to be sympathetic to Cnut; it was this promise of stability through military prowess that won him the surname 'Ironside'. However, Cnut too had mixed sources of support. Cnut had triumphed with the support of the Anglo-Saxon Eadric Streona and, at other times, other Anglo-Saxons had aided Viking invaders. The kind of England that would develop out of 1016 was going to be anything but straightforward.

CHAPTER 3

New King ... New Broom ...

The impact of Cnut's consolidation of power: 1016–25

In this chapter we will examine the early years of the reign of Cnut, 1016–c.1025. As we shall see, after Cnut took power in England he purged the Anglo-Saxon elites; we will identify who was purged and why, and the impact of this on the power politics of the eleventh century. This is very important as the ripples from this 'rock' that Cnut's purges threw into the political 'pond' of Anglo-Saxon England had long-term implications; fifty years later their repercussions were still impacting on England when the events that initially caused them were long forgotten. Given that Cnut's 'Viking Conquest' was so significant, we shall also look at the nature of Cnut's rule as he settled into power as King of England as well as King of Denmark. Since this drew England ever closer into the rivalries, ambitions and wars of Scandinavia, the nature of his Anglo-Danish Empire in this period also needs to be examined, along with any implications for future 'Viking entanglements' that might ensue.

A Viking king of England and Denmark

Despite the fact that the Danish Viking, Svein Forkbeard, had briefly held the throne of England until his death in February 1014, it was really his son Cnut's accession to the English throne in 1016 that truly marked the Danish 'Viking Conquest' of England. Following the death of Edmund Ironside in November 1016, Cnut united the kingdoms of England and Denmark. This formed an Anglo-Danish North Sea Empire, which occasionally also included the kingdom of Norway and extended its influence into Sweden. As a result, the united kingdom of England was now ruled not by a member of the West Saxon line, descended from its legendary fifth-century ancestor Cerdic, but instead by a Viking king who owed his crown not to birthright but to conquest and military prowess.

However, the creation of this single Anglo-Danish kingdom had not, it seems, been the intention of Svein Forkbeard. Svein had two sons – Cnut and Harald – and divided up his empire between them. Harald, the elder, was given Denmark; Cnut was given the wealthier inheritance of England, but securing this was far from certain. A bird in the hand

(Denmark) was worth more than one in the bush (England), even if the latter had the potential to be the really big prize.

After Svein's death in 1014, Cnut had attempted to maintain Danish rule in England but been forced to return to Denmark by resistance to Viking rule across England. It is unclear exactly what Cnut expected to happen on his return home, where his brother was on the throne: while in England, Cnut had ordered coin-dies cut as if he expected to issue coins in his own name in Denmark too. Clearly, the family reunion of brothers in Denmark had the potential to be anything but harmonious. The *Encomium Emmae Reginae* (*In Praise of Queen Emma*) states that Cnut wanted to rule Denmark jointly with his brother but that Harald – unsurprisingly – refused.[1] This account presents Cnut as the wise brother and Harald as the unwise.

The *Encomium* was written by a monk living in St Omer, in what is now France; it was composed during the reign of Cnut's son, Harthacnut (ruled England 1040–42). It details the life of Cnut's queen, Emma, and was commissioned by her in the turbulent period at the end of the Anglo-Danish rule, when Cnut's death had led to a power struggle between his own two sons (*see* Chapter 6). Consequently, the matter of brotherly power-sharing may have influenced the *Encomium*'s writer's view of the earlier dynastic dispute between Cnut and his brother: he may have wanted to underline the problems that arose when brothers would not share. In his view the earlier arrangement had not revealed fraternal unity and peace, and this may have been due to him reading back into the past his experiences from his own time.

The *Encomium*'s account may also have been coloured by the later situation in which Harthacnut (who had no heir) decided to cooperate with his half-brother Edward the Confessor (their mother, Emma of Normandy, had been married in turn to both Æthelred II and Cnut). In this context, the playing up of problems caused by earlier sibling rivalry may have been intended to discourage a later outbreak of the same problem. On the other hand, the earlier arrangement may not necessarily have been initially fraught with difficulty. This is because, although not common, sharing the ruling of a kingdom was not unheard of, and the later King Magnus of Norway (ruled 1035–47) would briefly share the throne with his uncle, Harald Hardrada. The latter would be a key player in the events of autumn 1066. But this is to digress from Cnut.

What seems clear is that – whatever the initial likelihood of the arrangement working harmoniously – Cnut's apparent ambition to share the Danish throne was, in the end, frustrated by his brother's reluctance to cooperate when it was required. With Harald refusing to share power, Cnut had two options: fight Harald for control of Denmark, or take England. He chose the second option and so, in 1015, he launched his invasion of England. He became sole king there after the death of

Edmund Ironside in 1016. Very little is known about the reign of Cnut's brother, Harald, back in Denmark and his death is not actually recorded in the sparse Danish records. It seems likely that he died at some point in 1018 because in 1019 Cnut returned to Denmark and became King of Denmark as well as of England. In this move he united the two kingdoms into an Anglo-Danish Viking Empire of the North.

Cnut's early years in England: a Viking purge

When Cnut finally secured the whole of the kingdom of England, in 1017, following Edmund Ironside's death in 1016, he split the kingdom into four earldoms: Wessex, Mercia, East Anglia and Northumbria. He initially kept Wessex as royal land, though it was later given to Earl Godwin. Mercia was granted to Eadric Streona; East Anglia went to Thorkell the Tall; and Northumbria was given to Eric, Earl of Lade (in Norway).

Thorkell the Tall and Eric were allies of Cnut. We have come across Thorkell in Chapter 2 – he was associated with the legendary *Jómsvikings*, an elite community of warriors who had their base at Jomsborg on the southern coast of the Baltic. Thorkell, according to later traditions, took part in the semi-legendary sea-battle of *Hjörungavágr* in 986, fought between the *Jómsvikings* and the Norwegian Earl of Lade (whose power-base was centred on Trondheim in Norway). Thorkell went on to fight other battles in Scandinavia and England. He went over to the side of King Æthelred II following the murder of the Archbishop of Canterbury by drunken warriors ostensibly under Thorkell's authority in 1012, but at some point between 1013 and 1017 he switched sides again and ended up serving Cnut and benefiting from this new alliance. It is possible that Thorkell only went over to Cnut on the death of Æthelred, or even as late as the final victory of Cnut. We cannot be sure: some historians have suggested that Thorkell actually played a key role in masterminding the accession of Cnut.[2]

Eric, Earl of Lade, also known as Eric Haakonsson, also features in later (semi-legendary) accounts and was another fearsome northern warrior. The illegitimate son of Haakon Sigurdarson – who ruled Norway under the authority of the King of Denmark, was allegedly descended from giants and was eventually murdered by his slave while hiding in a pig sty – Eric Haakonsson also fought at the battle of *Hjörungavágr*, although on the opposite side to Thorkell the Tall. As a twelve-year-old he allegedly hunted down and killed a warrior who had humiliated him and went on to rule in Norway, under the overlordship of the King of Denmark. His support for Cnut's invasion of England was rewarded with the earldom of Northumbria, which he held until his death, sometime between 1023 and 1033.

Despite these appointments of strong men to key positions, Cnut's accession to power was by no means straightforward and, as a conquering foreign figure, he needed to act swiftly and firmly to take control of England. This resulted in the start of Cnut's reign being characterized by executions and banishments. The *Anglo-Saxon Chronicle* entry for 1016 lists the major figures slain by Cnut. The first is Eadric Streona, whose double-crossing finally caught up with him: he was killed on Cnut's orders, even though he had finally chosen the Danish side. In the *F* manuscript of the *Chronicle* we are told that he was 'very rightly' killed, and John of Worchester – in the twelfth-century compilation, *Chronicon ex Chronicis (Chronicle of other Chronicles)* – reports that his corpse was thrown over the city walls of London where it was left unburied.[3] Eadric Streona's frequent side-swapping had not ended up as he had intended.

Eadric was not the only Anglo-Saxon nobleman to be swept away in the purge at the start of Cnut's reign. The *Chronicle* also records that Northman, the son of Ealdorman Leofwine, along with Æthelweard, son of Æthelmaer the Stout (who was ealdorman of the 'western provinces') and Brihtic, son of Ælfheah of Devon, were also killed at this time. Leofwine would later lead one of the most powerful families in England under Cnut, so clearly he managed to overcome any resentment he harboured concerning the execution of his son.

This was not the end of Cnut's purge. In 1020, another Æthelweard, Ealdorman Æthelweard, was outlawed. This was done at a large royal council held in Cirencester at Easter on Cnut's return from Denmark, where he had been securing the Danish throne for himself following his brother's death. It is unclear exactly why Æthelweard was expelled, but is likely it was linked to behaviour during Cnut's absence. There has been some suggestion that this period witnessed the return of the ætheling Eadwig (brother of Edmund Ironside) from exile, but there is no definite evidence to prove this. What is clear is that the top layer of the Anglo-Saxon aristocracy had been brutally thinned out. Ealdormen were important local magnates. In earlier times they had administered the shires (such as Wiltshire and Lincolnshire) for the crown, but by the eleventh century their power had increased and many had jurisdiction over a number of shires as earls.[4] Essentially, by the eleventh century, they 'wielded power not over discrete units of administration, but across fluctuating spheres of authority, the bounds of which changed according to the king's will.'[5]

The royal family was not immune from this purge. In 1017, the ætheling Eadwig was exiled and later murdered on Cnut's orders.[6] Eadwig was the fifth son of Æthelred II and was by now the last surviving son of his father's first marriage. John of Worcester reports that, in 1016, the English nobles exiled Eadwig and that Cnut, delighted by this, promised to reward a nobleman named Æthelweard if he murdered Eadwig.

This may well have been the same Æthelweard (son of Æthelmaer the Stout) who was murdered by Cnut in 1017. He, however, refused and the *Chronicle* records Eadwig's eventual banishment in 1017. However, this does not seem to have been the last of Eadwig, and he later appears to have returned to England – maybe in 1019 – possibly to try for the throne. For this, he paid with his life; manuscript C of the *Chronicle* tells us that Cnut later had Eadwig killed, and John of Worcester adds that it was those dearest to him who betrayed him.

This episode illustrates two of the reasons that might lie behind a person being swept up in Cnut's purge. In the case of Æthelweard it was not being loyal *enough*. Clearly, those members of the nobility in England who insisted on ætheling Eadwig's exile had made a judgement between his impeccable royal credentials (he was, after all, unquestionably of the royal bloodline) and the political reality of Cnut's occupation of the English throne backed by the might of Denmark! In the circumstances it was probably not that difficult a decision: Cnut's position was a *fait accompli* so the abandonment of Eadwig was an exercise in *Realpolitik*. But it was not enough. Æthelweard's enthusiasm for Cnut was tested beyond this and – from Cnut's perspective – was found wanting. Clearly, for men such as Æthelweard it was one thing to abandon a man such as Eadwig but quite another to actively connive in his death. Cnut did not see it that way. And so Æthelweard died because he was not loyal enough. One wonders if many of the others died for similar reasons. If they did, we should not assume that they were actively engaged in opposition to the new regime. They did not have to have had a track record to compare with the serial turncoat Eadric Streona; it may simply have been that they lacked enthusiasm or that they did not 'fit' in some other way.

The second reason for becoming a victim was having too much royal blood: as in later Tudor England, this could be very dangerous indeed. Ætheling Eadwig was a dead man walking simply because of his impeccable royal credentials. As long as he lived, a viable alternative to Cnut was available. If he added political ambition (the likely reason for a return in 1019) to this, then his fate was doubly sealed. However, the likelihood that Cnut planned for something unfortunate to happen to him while he was in exile – an event frustrated by Æthelweard's lack of compliance – indicates that even keeping out of the way offered no assurance of safety. Cnut had a long reach and was taking no chances: had Eadwig remained abroad he may still have found himself the victim of an accident that had been ordered by Cnut. The evidence for assuming that this would have been the case lies in how far from England the sons of Edmund Ironside had to be sent in order to be safe from the reach of Cnut, as we shall now see.

The young children of Edmund Ironside (the æthelings Edward and Edmund) were also at risk. The 1057 entry in the *Chronicle* tells us that

Cnut had them banished to Hungary. This story is also recorded by John of Worcester, who further informs us that they were first sent to the king of Sweden for him to kill. Reluctant to do so, he instead sent them to Solomon, king of the Hungarians, the plan being for Solomon to bring them up in his court.[7] This tale of travel and intrigue will be explored in more depth in Chapter 7, but does tell us something of the very nominal control Cnut had over the King of Sweden in this period: Cnut's political influence had its limits. John of Worcester adds that it was the treacherous Eadric Streona who advised Cnut to murder the æthelings,[8] though this may well have been an attempt to apportion blame for a planned crime, which – even by eleventh-century standards – was clearly abhorrent, onto a man whose character had already been irretrievably blackened.

Another man exiled at this time was enigmatically described as Eadwig 'king of the peasants'. This is a very strange title but he is referred to in this way in both the *Chronicle* entry for 1017 (in Old English *ceorlacyng*) and by the twelfth-century historians John of Worcester and Henry of Huntingdon (in the Latin form *rex rusticorum*). We unfortunately know virtually nothing else about this man, or why he was given this strange title.[9] It is possible that he was the leader of a peasant rising, and the difficult conditions towards the end of Æthelred II's reign may well have provided the perfect backdrop for this. John of Worcester does tell us, though, that Eadwig 'king of the peasants' was later reconciled with Cnut. He should not, of course, be confused with ætheling Eadwig, the murdered royal.

The Cnut-purge was not simply confined to the English elite: Scandinavian leaders who had helped Cnut to claim the throne also found themselves victims. One of the most prominent of these was Thorkell the Tall. As we have seen, Thorkell's early history is steeped in tales of the *Jómsvikings*, the semi-legendary band of Viking mercenaries prominent in the tenth and eleventh centuries. Thorkell was a Viking warlord to be reckoned with; he is reported as having taken part in a number of significant naval battles in Scandinavia in the late tenth century, but his association with England started in 1010 when he landed near Ipswich, defeating the local army and eventually being paid an unusually large tribute (*gafol*) in 1011. He then changed sides and went into the service of Æthelred II against Svein Forkbeard and Cnut, but at some point he went back to Denmark, returning to England in the service of Cnut. Like Eadric Streona, Thorkell was a powerful leader who commanded his own men and was not adverse to switching sides; he had his own agenda and the necessary means to carry it out. Given this, it is perhaps not surprising that, although Thorkell was initially rewarded by Cnut in 1017, they later fell out. Unlike Eadric Streona, though, Thorkell was expelled rather than executed, and he was reconciled with Cnut the following year.

The difference in the treatment of Thorkell and Eadric is easily explained. Eadric was a self-serving political operator whose track-record inspired no confidence regarding his future actions. He was a loose cannon and Cnut was not going to wait until Eadric next decided his own interests took his 'loyalty' elsewhere. Thorkell was different. He was an independent Viking lord, cut from the same cloth as Svein Fork-beard and Cnut himself. He had his own mind, but there is no reason to consider him inherently unreliable. Even his switching of sides in the last period of the Viking Wars can be explained as a principled reaction to the murder of the Archbishop of Canterbury – an atrocity at which even a Viking drew the line. And he had a following. As a result, Cnut handled him more carefully. In 1019, Thorkell even acted as regent in England when Cnut returned to Denmark that year.

The circumstances of Thorkell's ultimate fall are surprising. In 1021, he was outlawed and banished by Cnut. We lack detailed contemporary evidence regarding this, but later sources claim that Thorkell's wife was found guilty of poisoning his son by his first marriage, a murder that also involved an accusation of witchcraft on her part. Thorkell had sworn an oath regarding her innocence and was badly compromised. From Cnut's point of view this all sounds just too convenient, and there is every likeli-hood that this was a royally instigated show-trial designed to blacken the reputation of Thorkell via his wife and following the death of his son. The accusations of poisoning and witchcraft sound as if they had been carefully crafted in order to achieve maximum impact on an over-mighty subject. However, Thorkell seems to have maintained enough of a mili-tary following to force Cnut to return to Denmark in 1022 in order to deal with the threat he posed there. Eventually, in 1023, Cnut appointed Thorkell as his deputy in Denmark as the price of their reconciliation.[10] After this, Thorkell vanishes from history. He may have died soon after 1023 or he may have had an 'accident' organized by Cnut. We do not know.

Thorkell was not the only Scandinavian to find that his early elevation by Cnut was rapidly followed by a surprisingly negative *denouement*. Henry of Huntingdon and William of Malmesbury – both twelfth-century English historians – state that Eric of Lade (the Earl of Northumbria) was eventually exiled and John of Worcester – another twelfth-century English historian – suggests that his son was expelled with him. What we can say for certain is that Eric signed his last charter in 1023, although later Norwegian and Icelandic sources suggest Eric died in England.

In addition to these victims, tradition suggests that Cnut had his brother-in-law, Úlf, murdered in the church in Roskilde, Denmark, on Christmas Day 1026. Cnut was a dangerous person to fall out with or be perceived as a threat by.

These developments reveal something of a pattern: an early accommodation with powerful players who are then brought down, to be replaced (as we shall later see) by men either wholly dependent on Cnut or perceived as offering no threat to his power. After Thorkell's fall, we hear of no Earl of East Anglia until Harold Godwinson was appointed to that position in 1045. Given the importance of East Anglia in the eleventh century – in terms of population density and economic importance – this is significant: a wealthy area was being kept out of the hands of potential rivals. We do not hear of another earl holding southern Northumbria until 1033, when one named Siward appears in that position; he did not hold northern Northumbria until 1041. Many of Cnut's earls are 'little more than names',[11] in charge of areas of reduced size compared with their immediate predecessors. It was not until the 1030s (*see* Chapter 4) that Cnut revised this policy and allowed the rise of Leofric of Mercia and Godwin of Wessex, with greatly expanded spheres of influence. By that time he clearly felt that he had destroyed anyone capable of threatening his position.

Those named above were just the tip of the iceberg. The *Encomium* states that many English leaders were killed at the same time as Eadric Streona. Similarly, the later *Evesham Chronicle* reports that many of Eadric's soldiers were killed with him.[12] This would fit with records from the eleventh-century Durham tract *De Obsessione Dunelmi* (*On the siege of Durham*), which states that forty men were killed alongside Uhtred of Northumbria in 1016. Uhtred also seems to have been murdered on the orders of Cnut although the details of his life and death are frustratingly few and far between. Writing after the Norman Conquest, William of Poitiers states that Cnut slaughtered the 'noblest of England's sons' to secure his position on the throne. What is certain is that Cnut was a ruthless man, who was well aware of the various threats posed to his rule. He was also a man who lived in dangerous and violent times and, while this string of executions was undoubtedly brutal and may seem shocking by modern standards, they were part of the way of life – particularly Scandinavian – in the eleventh century.

The combination of the large number of men slain at the Battle of Ashingdon in 1016, in which we are told by the *Chronicle* the 'flower of England perished', with the purges at the beginning of Cnut's reign, had a devastating effect on the Anglo-Saxon elites. Cnut was cleansing himself of threats both from those who represented the old English order but also from those Scandinavian earls and warlords who had been powerful and successful in the attacks on Æthelred's England. Cnut was about to create a new order that gained legitimacy neither from its ancient ties to England nor to proven military prowess, but one that was dependent first and foremost on him. This would help to ease the transition from the Anglo-Saxon royal line of Cerdic to that of the Danes as represented by Cnut, and would also help to eliminate the potential threat from the other Viking warlords who had attacked England alongside Svein and Cnut.

Cnut's consolidation of power in England: an astute marriage

Another strategy used by Cnut to ease the transition from the old to the new regime was his marriage to the widow of Æthelred II (and daughter of the Duke of Normandy), Emma. Cnut already had a wife 'in the Danish fashion' as it was termed at the time. This was Ælfgifu of Northampton – more an 'unofficial wife' than a mistress – with whom he had two sons. However, in 1017, he ordered that Emma should be fetched from Normandy to become his wife.* William of Jumièges – a late eleventh-century Norman historian – records Cnut as having married Emma after having her brought from London while it was under siege in 1016. However, his chronology does not appear to be accurate and it seems more likely that the marriage took place later, in 1017. This is more likely, as by then Edmund Ironside was dead, Cnut had the crown and consolidation of power was the order of the day. The *Encomium* records Cnut's men as fetching Emma back from Normandy, but the renowned Anglo-Saxonist Simon Keynes has suggested she may have remained in England throughout. What is in no doubt, however, is that Cnut married her.

There was something of an age difference between them; Cnut was twenty-one while Emma was about thirty-one. In addition, Cnut's taking of the throne had led to the exile and loss of royal birthright of her two sons by Æthelred II (æthelings Edward and Alfred). Despite these factors, the marriage seems to have worked well and resulted in the birth of another son, Harthacnut. Marrying Emma neutralized the threat posed by her two sons by Æthelred II and prevented them from mounting a bid for the English throne with Norman assistance.[13] We may assume that there was an exchange of emissaries between Cnut and Richard of Normandy, Emma's brother, prior to the marriage to ensure Richard's goodwill as well as that of his sister: a marriage to Emma without the agreement of her brother would only have assured Cnut of an unfriendly power just across the English Channel. And, furthermore, the exiled æthelings Edward and Alfred were sheltering with their Norman relatives. This potentially dangerous situation needed attention. The fact that Cnut later married off his own sister, Estrith, to Richard of Normandy's

---

*Emma is the Norman version, while in Old English her name is Ælgifu. To differentiate the two women, Queen Ælfgifu will be referred to as Emma, while Ælfgifu of Northampton will be given her English name.

successor, Robert, is likely proof that marriage to Emma alone was not sufficient to defuse the Norman danger.

Emma was a remarkable and politically astute woman. Due to her commissioning the *Encomium Emmae Reginae*, she is one of the few early medieval women whose life we know about in some detail. She was to outlive both of her husbands and live to see two of her sons – Harthacnut, her son by Cnut, and Edward the Confessor, her son by Æthelred II – become kings of England.

The virtue of peace

The acceptance of Cnut as king did not result in an immediate end to the payment of *heregeld* (the army-tax often referred to as *Danegeld*). In 1018, a tribute was paid all over England of £82,500 to pay off Cnut's army; as a result, only forty ships remained with Cnut while the rest returned to Denmark. This was to be the last of the great Viking-related payments and is linked in the *Chronicle* with a reference to the English (Anglo-Saxons) and the Danes meeting at Oxford and coming to a political understanding. A document produced after the meeting, by Archbishop Wulfstan of York, claimed that all differences between the two sides were set aside and that, consequently, peace and friendship was established. These two sources of evidence indicate that the meeting at Oxford, in 1018, was truly significant and that it finally established an enduring understanding between the two sides. There were to be no more Viking raids during Cnut's reign.

The accession of Cnut brought peace to England. For most ordinary people the fact that they were being ruled by a Dane meant very little: the more important feature of his rule was that it had ended the turbulence and devastation that had characterized Æthelred II's reign. A Viking victory had, at last, brought an end to the crisis caused by the Vikings, and one might cynically argue that, having done most to bring violence and disruption to England since the 990s, the Scandinavian poacher had become head gamekeeper! Not only this, but this particular 'head gamekeeper' was not going to put up with the disloyalty (and attendant instability and military weakness) that had so seriously undermined the reigns of his two Anglo-Saxon predecessors.

The opportunities for treachery that had occurred as a result of the Viking Wars were to be terminated, and swiftly. This increased political stability was a clear outcome of Cnut's 'peace dividend' that resulted from his conquest. If anyone doubted this they had only to recall the salutary lesson of Eadric Streona: in line with eleventh-century values, the cutting short of a political career involved the cutting short of the political actor. The lesson was dramatic and unambiguous.

The agreement with the Anglo-Saxon elites that occurred at Oxford did not, however, immediately end all political tension. That Cnut's temporary return to Denmark in 1020 was followed by the exile of Ealdorman Æthelweard of Wessex suggests that Cnut's absence had led to unrest in England, although not enough to threaten his rule. The fact that Cnut was able to return safely to Denmark again in 1023 and again in 1026 also suggests that his grip on the country was fairly tight. While Cnut's accession to the throne was by no means without its bumps and complications, he certainly did not encounter the organized rebellion experienced by William the Conqueror fifty years later. It is unclear exactly why this was so, although Cnut's pre-emptive strikes against both Anglo-Saxon and Scandinavian elites may help to account for it. It may also have been that, for the Anglo-Danish population of the north and east of England at least, a new king from Denmark was acceptable given the peculiarly Scandinavian character of the Danelaw.

What is clear is that, alongside the elite purges, occurred the establishment of a stability that would have affected the lives of most ordinary Anglo-Saxons and, in time, all members of the English aristocracy who had escaped the purges and who were nimble-footed enough to accommodate the change of regime. The 'Pax-Cnut' was not without its losers but, undoubtedly, there were more winners in this new situation, in terms of beneficiaries of peace and stability.

What did Cnut do next?

By 1020, Cnut seems to have secured a relatively firm grip on England. Following the meeting at Cirencester at which Ealdorman Æthelweard was expelled, Cnut travelled to Ashingdon for the consecration of the church that commemorated the 1016 battle. It seems likely that this visit coincided with the anniversary of the battle on 18 October. The consecration of the church was performed by Wulfstan, the Archbishop of York. This is the same Wulfstan who was author of the famous *Sermo Lupi ad Anglos* (*Sermon of the Wolf to the English*), which had earlier admonished the English for their crimes and linked these to the renewed Viking attacks in Æthelred II's reign. After this point, detailed information about Cnut's activities dramatically decreases. The *Chronicle* entry for 1021 simply outlines the outlawing of Earl Thorkell the Tall, while the 1022 entry records that Cnut sailed with his ships to *Wiht* or *Witland*; this is commonly thought to refer to the Isle of Wight.

We have already explored the first of these occurrences but the second is worth examining in a little more detail. It is unclear exactly what happened in 1022 to mean that Cnut needed to place his navy at the Isle of Wight. It has been suggested this positioning has a Norman link, given that this is where Harold Godwinson's forces waited for the Normans in the summer of 1066. However, a Norman threat to southern England, countered by Cnut moving his fleet to the Isle of Wight, seems unlikely as Cnut appears to have been on good terms with Richard of Normandy. Alternatively, it may have been in response to pirate raids such as those experienced in 1018 and 1047. There has even been some suggestion that it does not refer to the Isle of Wight at all and, instead, *Witland* refers to an area of north-east Poland: this would link to Henry of Huntingdon's tale of Cnut fighting against the Slavs. However, on balance, the Isle of Wight seems a more likely option as both the *C* and *E* manuscripts of the *Chronicle* refer to the destination as *Wiht* (Wight), while it is only the later *D* manuscript that calls it *Witland*.

Whatever Cnut's movements in 1022, in 1023 he returned to Denmark. On his return to England, he appears to have been accompanied by the Bishop of Roskilde, who was brought back to be consecrated by the Archbishop of Canterbury. In June Cnut was in London for the translation of St Ælfheah from St Paul's to Canterbury; the saint was the Archbishop Ælfheah who had been murdered by Thorkell the Tall's men in 1012, having refused to allow himself to be ransomed. Cnut's involvement in this cult may well have been politically motivated, an opportunity to atone for the sins of his countrymen and to neutralize any potential unrest the translation could have led to. This would be one of Cnut's first steps to ingratiate himself into English culture and English traditions. Cnut may have held onto his throne in the early years through executions and banishments but, in time, he would make his hold secure by becoming more English than the English.

Cnut's Scandinavian Empire

While England was clearly the jewel in Cnut's crown, it should not be forgotten that Cnut ruled over a North Sea Empire that at times encompassed not only England but also Denmark and Norway, and whose influence stretched into Sweden. Although much is known about the rule of Cnut in England, the relative paucity of written source material from Scandinavia during this period means that there is surprisingly little known about his rule in Denmark. Denmark had only very recently become an officially Christian country – the conversion having taken place under Cnut's grandfather, Harald Bluetooth – and since literacy and Christianity tended to go hand-in-hand, there is very little in terms of contemporary written source material.

One of the main questions regarding Cnut's rule is exactly how he organized the government of Denmark given how little time he spent there. Was there one person left in charge? Did he appoint several earls in the way in which he had split England into four earldoms? The *Chronicle* does inform us that Thorkell the Tall was entrusted with the governing of Denmark in 1023. However, there is no further mention of him in the records and it may be seriously doubted as to whether he actually made it to become regent of Denmark. It may have been that he was simply too old for further military service and lived out his final days in retirement, or that he fell out with Cnut again and was expelled from the kingdom. Alternatively, he may simply have died soon after his appointment as regent of Denmark.

It does appear, though, that less than three years later there was another regent in Denmark. This time it was Earl Úlf, another of Cnut's campaigning companions; he is believed to have been the husband of Cnut's sister Estrith and the father of Svein Estrithson, the future king of Denmark. Adam of Bremen tells that that Úlf was a 'duke' in England. Adam was the late-eleventh-century monk from the bishopric of Hamburg-Bremen (in modern Germany) who wrote a history of the church there, entitled *Gesta Hammaburgensis Ecclesiae Pontificum* (*Deeds of the Archbishops of Hamburg*). Hamburg-Bremen was responsible for the conversion of Scandinavia and this caused Adam to include some information about Scandinavia in his writing. His account has led some modern scholars to suggest that Úlf was English, though this seems highly unlikely since none of his relatives have English names. His father was named Thorgils, his brother was named Eilif, his sons were named Bjorn and Svein, and his sister was named Gytha. It is likely that Úlf was Danish but had been granted land in England by Cnut.

As will be explored further in Chapter 4, Úlf's promotion was not successful and he did not meet a happy end. Saxo Grammaticus records he was assassinated in Roskilde church at Christmas 1026. Saxo was a late-twelfth/early-thirteenth-century Danish historian, theologian and author who wrote the first history of Denmark, the *Gesta Danorum* (*Deeds of the Danes*). So it seems that Cnut's purging tendencies were not just limited to English earls. After this point however, it becomes less clear who was in charge of Denmark in Cnut's absence.

Although he was the King of Denmark, Cnut spent surprisingly little time there, visiting only four times during his reign. Despite this, he did exercise political authority and control over the country and this can be clearly seen in the military support that he was able to attract for his conquest of Norway. Another sign of the support that Cnut was able to muster can be seen in the expansion of several Danish towns during his reign. The town of Viborg, in central Jutland, seems to have undergone a series of adjustments along the settlement's north side. A stone wall was constructed with a series of plots laid out alongside and houses parallel to them. This extensive reorganization seems to have occurred during the reign of Cnut and the extent of it suggests that it happened at the command of Cnut. In addition, although dating evidence from the cemetery in Lund raises doubts as to whether Cnut was responsible for the foundation of the town in 1020, the building around the cemetery can be dated to 1020, which suggests an extension of the town under Cnut. This would indicate that, despite Cnut's frequent absences, he still maintained some form of direct control over Denmark. However, these absences must have had an effect on the nature of his rule and, although he did exercise political authority, the fact that he spent most of his reign in England rather than Denmark must mean that Cnut acted as more of an overlord in Denmark than as a hands-on king.

After Cnut had gained control of Denmark, he became concerned about relationships with his Scandinavian neighbours including Norway, Sweden, the German empire and the Slav peoples living east of the river Elbe. After the death of Olaf Tryggvason – King of Norway – in c.1000, the kingdom was ruled by the Norwegian Earl of Lade under the over-lordship of Svein Forkbeard. However, Danish domination did not last. The defeat of the Earl of Lade by Olaf Haraldsson at the Battle of Nesjar, in 1015, meant that Cnut lost control over Norway. Cnut suffered another serious setback in Scandinavia with the death of the Swedish king, Olaf, in 1022. Olaf had been an ally of Cnut: Adam of Bremen tells us that he had a treaty with Cnut, and that Cnut had planned his conquest of England with Olaf's help and had the support of Olaf for further Danish expansion into Norway. This meant that Cnut's position in Scandinavia was significantly weakened by Olaf's death.

The most important consequence of Cnut's Northern Empire was that it increased the connection of England to the complex politics of Scandi-navia. This would continue to be the case throughout Cnut's reign (as we shall see in Chapter 4) and also in the reigns of his sons Harald Harefoot and Harthacnut. This involvement would continue to affect England as far as 1066 and beyond.

The consequences of Cnut's first few years

Anglo-Saxon England had been put under enormous social and political strain through two hundred years of Viking raids, which had increased in the period immediately before 1016. In addition to the upheavals in the last years of Æthelred II's reign and the beginning of Cnut's, the three most important earls in the kingdom, Uhtred of Northumbria, Eadric of Mercia and Ulfcetel of East Anglia, along with Ælfric of Hampshire and Godwine of Lindsey, all died during this last phase of the Viking Wars. Furthermore, the *Chronicle* records that seven important thegns (lesser nobles) also died in battle, through assassination, or execution. The attri-tion continued during Cnut's purges. Therefore, although many of the elite under Cnut were Anglo-Saxons, very few of these were from the

same families that had previously ruled the English regions for generations. The established class of practitioners of traditional Anglo-Saxon
regional government, with all its attendant system of local patronage and
obligation, had been shattered by the wars and by Cnut's purges. This
was accompanied by an increased involvement of England in the politics
of Viking Scandinavia.

CHAPTER 4

New Men and New Opportunities

The Viking impact on England: undermining the system of government

As we have seen in Chapter 3, Cnut's reign brought with it a clearing out of the old order and the creation of new men. This meant that the balance of power had shifted in England, leading to the destabilization of the established English political system. It can be argued that the results of the seismic shift brought about by the Danish conquest would be felt long after the last Danish king sat on the English throne, and ultimately created the backdrop for the more enduring Norman conquest of England.

However, to lay the blame for this weakening of the English political system solely at Cnut's door would not be entirely fair, as there were several long-term factors that also contributed. It was not just Cnut's accession to the throne but also the renewed Viking attacks of the last fifty years and in particular the invasion and conquest of England by Cnut's father, Svein Forkbeard, that led to the weakening of the rule of the royal house of Wessex. These were, nevertheless, all Viking-related causes.

The usual characteristics of a lawful Anglo-Saxon royal succession were: eligibility by birth (royal blood), designation by the late king (royal selection), recognition by the leading elites (acclamation) and consecration by the Church (making holy by religious ceremony). Normally the eldest son of the previous king succeeded to the throne. However, a king might nominate different men as his heir at different points in time, and the different regions within England could make different choices as to who should succeed. In addition, consecration sometimes did not occur. It is noteworthy that the *Anglo-Saxon Chronicle* does not mention the coronation of any of the Anglo-Danish kings. It does, though, record the consecrations of Æthelred II and Edward the Confessor.[1] So, things were flexible but certain ingredients were expected: a close blood-connection to the royal line and acceptance by the Anglo-Saxon elites.

To the Viking-related causes of instability should be added some home-grown ingredients. The murder of Edward King and Martyr by other Anglo-Saxons in 978 had allowed his younger brother Æthelred II to come to the throne, and the treachery and weakness of Æthelred II's reign helped to undermine the support-base of the royal house. Archbishop Wulfstan's *Sermo Lupi ad Anglos* (*Sermon of the Wolf to the English*) was a polemic that was finished in about 1014, and declared the idea that the Viking raids were divine retribution for the behaviour of the English. Among the many and various crimes that Wulfstan lists as leading to the Vikings' violent onslaught, the murder of Edward is picked out for particular condemnation and it is described in Old English as '*Ealra mæst hlaforswice se bið on worulde*' ('A full, the greatest treachery there is in the world').[2] So, even before Cnut conquered England in 1016, the traditional legitimacy of the Anglo-Saxon monarchy had been weakened. This could have been reversed with a succession of kings like Edmund Ironside, but this was not to be and the Viking Conquest of 1016 completed this demolition job.

In addition, during the unrest and confusion at the end of Æthelred II's reign, the leading Anglo-Saxon nobles became accustomed to having an increased role in the choosing of kings. This saw itself in the acceptance of Svein Forkbeard as king in 1013 and then in the swift abandonment of his successor, Cnut, when Æthelred II returned from exile in 1014; then groups formed around Edmund Ironside to champion his cause while Æthelred II still lived; and finally, throne-worthy Anglo-Saxons were passed over as the elites accepted the inevitable and threw their support behind Cnut in 1016–17 after the death of Edmund Ironside. While the Anglo-Saxon elites had accepted the various kings that were presented to them, they seem to have felt that they still had a role to play in the process.[3] As a result, the events accompanying the seizure of power by Viking Danish kings had raised the expectations of the English political elites regarding their own role in the royal succession, and this coincided with a period of weakening of the accepted legitimacy of the ruling Anglo-Saxon royal family.

An unexpected Viking legacy: a new elite class

The clearing out of the old order by Cnut left a vacuum that needed to be filled, and from this wreckage the earls Godwin, Leofric and Siward emerged. These new earls were the political descendants of the powerful ealdormen (the king's regional representatives) who had governed Anglo-Saxon England under royal authority since the ninth century. They were, however, largely drawn from 'new' families.

Originally each ealdorman had administrative responsibility for a single shire (the equivalent of a modern county). However, after West Saxon kings seized land lost to Viking settlers in eastern England in the tenth century, the ealdormen's role expanded to cover groups of shires. In the reign of Cnut their title was replaced by that of earl (a title related to the Norse word for a senior nobleman, a *jarl*). The new earldoms did not have fixed boundaries, and different ones were sometimes combined and then broken up. Any combination of adjacent shires might be combined to form an earldom by the mid-eleventh century. During the reign of Edward the Confessor there were usually nine earldoms at any one time, although sometimes they were without an earl and so under direct royal administration for periods of time.

Under Cnut there were major changes in the political landscape of English regional government, and this affected the political balance of power generally across the country. In the Midlands and the north, the new earls Siward and Leofric held the 'old' regional powerbases of Northumbria and Mercia; however, another 'new man', Godwin, was appointed as the first Earl of Wessex. This role had previously not existed as Wessex had always been held by the crown, since the kings of England, until now, had all been from the West Saxon royal house. However, since Cnut had no particular attachment to Wessex, there was no reason not to create an Earl of Wessex to sit alongside the earls of Northumbria, Mercia and East Anglia. It is interesting, though, that this was a later appointment and that initially Cnut did keep Wessex for himself.

All of these men were 'new man', made by Cnut. Godwin is not found in English sources before Cnut's reign and it seems that his father, Wulfnoth Cild of Sussex, was the rebel against Æthelred II mentioned by the *Chronicle* in 1009.[4] The *Chronicle* records that Beorhtric, the brother of Eadric Streona, made an accusation against Wulfnoth to King Æthelred in 1009 – unjustly, according to John of Worcester – and Wulfnoth then fled with twenty ships and proceeded to harry the south coast. Beorhtric followed with eighty ships, but his fleet was driven ashore by a storm and burnt by Wulfnoth. After the loss of a third of the fleet the remaining ships were withdrawn to London, and the Vikings were able to invade Kent unopposed. It is highly likely that Æthelred confiscated Wulfnoth's property as a result. Under Cnut, things were taking a turn for the better for this family.

The next of these men was Leofric, who became Earl of Mercia. His father, Leofwine (died c.1028), was an ealdorman of an area called the Hwicce in Mercia and is recorded as witnessing a charter of Æthelred II in 997 where he is recorded as *Wicciarum Prouinciarum dux* (ealdorman of the Hwicce). This area was in modern Worcestershire, Gloucestershire, parts of Warwickshire, small parts of Herefordshire, Shropshire, Staffordshire and north-west Wiltshire. Leofwine is known to have had at least four children including Northman, who was reputedly a retainer of Eadric Streona and was one of those executed by Cnut in 1017. His brother's execution allowed for Leofric's rise to power. He is now perhaps most famous for being the husband of Lady Godiva who, according to legend, rode naked through Coventry in protest at the taxation levels her husband had imposed on his tenants. Compared with Godwin and Siward, who were very much new additions to the top tier of power, Leofric was 'old money'.

Siward, the Earl of Northumbria, was a Scandinavian with no previous English connections and who, therefore, owed his position solely to Cnut.[5] Cnut's elevation of Godwin, importing of Siward and promotion of Leofric created a new class of elites who both owed everything to the king and yet also wielded huge amounts of power. In fact, their power was unprecedented. When ætheling Edward (the future King Edward the Confessor) returned to England in 1042, the area that had been the heartland of his ancestors was now held by a new Anglo-Danish family. And it was a family that had been especially closely related to the regime of Cnut, since Godwin had married Gytha, the sister of the Danish earl, Úlf, who in turn was married to Cnut's sister, Estrith.

This was not a totally new process and was one that had started under the Anglo-Saxon King Athelstan in the tenth century, with the rise of powerful local men, such as one (another Athelstan, the ealdorman of East Anglia) who was so powerful that he was even described as 'Half-King'. This had continued under Æthelred II, with the rise of Eadric Streona, who had similarly been extremely influential. However, Godwin and his family were to become even mightier subjects than either of these earlier figures, which was directly attributable to the reign of Cnut and his sons and their style of rule. What had occurred earlier in a small number of examples became 'the system' under Cnut. It arose from his rule-by-conquest, since these new men were very much under his control and lacked the independence that might have come from generations of holding down powerful positions.

The rise of Godwin

While all of these earls were important, perhaps the most important new man was Earl Godwin of Wessex, father of Harald II Godwinson (king in 1066). In 1016, Godwin could not have dreamt of his son sitting on the throne of England, but fifty years later an extraordinary combination of events enabled this to happen.

Almost nothing is known of Godwin's early years, the author of the *Encomium Emmae* (from here on referred to as the encomiast) suggests Godwin's rise to power was a result of not only his wise counsel but also his military service to Cnut. Godwin rose quickly to prominence and, by 1018, he had received an earldom – the earldom of all or at least part of Wessex – and in 1019 he was married to Gytha, the king's sister-in-law. Gytha was the sister of Earl Úlf who we met in the previous chapter as the regent in Denmark and the father of the future Danish king, Svein Estrithson. Gytha bore Godwin at least nine children, six sons (Svein, Harold, Tostig, Gyrth, Leofwine and Wulfnoth) and three daughters (Edith, Gunnhild and Ælfgifu). The oldest of Godwin and Gytha's sons were all given Scandinavian names and this may well point to the family consciously viewing themselves as Anglo-Danish rather than Anglo-Saxon.[6] The encomiast describes Godwin as a good father who was dedicated to the education of his children, an education that focused on helping them to act as lieutenants to future kings.

One of the best sources of information about Godwin and his family is the *Vita Ædwardi Regis qui apud Westmonasterium Requiescit* (*Life of King Edward who rests at Westminster*). This was completed c.1067 and was commissioned by Queen Edith, the wife of Edward the Confessor and daughter of Godwin. The text is in two parts: the first deals with the events before the Norman conquest of 1066 and the history of the Godwin family, the second deals with the holiness of Edward the Confessor. The *Vita Ædwardi* records that Godwin was not only made an ealdorman but was made *bajulus* of almost the whole kingdom. It is likely this word is linked to the word 'bailiff' and signified the creation of a new position. What we know for certain is that by the end of Cnut's reign, Godwin was the premier nobleman in England and had a close relationship with Cnut.

Despite his prominence, there is surprisingly little that can be said about Godwin during the reign of Cnut. Some information can be gleaned from Cnut's charters, though. Anglo-Saxon charters typically made a grant of land or recorded a privilege. As well as providing a record of the land-grant, these documents also contain witness lists, and the ranking of noblemen within these witness lists can tell us a lot about who was in favour at court at the time these charters were produced. Godwin is consistently the first lay-witness named in Cnut's charters after 1023, which suggests that he had reached his position of pre-eminence by this point.

The evidence from a runestone in Scandinavia suggests that Godwin accompanied Cnut on at least one of his trips back to Denmark. The runestone erected to commemorate the death of one Bjor Arnsteinson records that he 'found his death in Godwin's host when Cnut sailed to England'. It is unclear which visit Godwin participated in: the *Vita Ædwardi* suggests it was Cnut's first visit, whereas William of Malmesbury – a twelfth-century historian – suggests that it was in fact the expedition of 1025, which included the Battle of Holy River. What does seem likely is that, if Godwin did remain in England in 1025, he was a man trusted to rule England in Cnut's absence. The lack of unrest in England during Cnut's long absences may well be a testament not only to Cnut's power but also to Godwin's abilities.

Tensions and politics – the rivalry between the earls of Wessex and the earls of Mercia

The creation of this new layer of powerful subjects by Cnut led to unprecedented factions and tensions within the elite. The rivalry between the earls of Mercia and the house of Godwin continued until the Norman Conquest: although there were periods when they did cooperate, this rivalry was a significant factor in English politics in this period of time. The author of the *Vita Ædwardi* referred to '*odia veteri*' (old hatreds) between the earls of Mercia and the house of Godwin. He was not exaggerating.

Knowledge of this hatred is essential background for any reading of the mid-eleventh-century annals in the *Chronicle*. For example, the annals found in manuscript C are anti-Godwin because they were written in Mercia by monks whose political sympathies lay with the earls of Mercia.[7] Manuscript C, for this period, contains nine annals containing anti-Godwin views and four that are concerned with the affairs of Abingdon (an important Mercian religious house). Another fifteen annals are concerned with Mercian affairs generally. Finally, seven are specifically interested in the family of Earl Leofric.[8] In contrast, manuscript E contains nine pro-Godwin annals, four annals concerned with the affairs of St Augustine's monastery in Canterbury and eight concerned with southern affairs generally. This is due to it being written at a location with greater sympathy and affiliation to Godwin and his family. A more neutral approach can be seen in manuscript D. This contains three annals concerned with the family of ætheling Edward the Exile (one of the sons of Edmund Ironside), fifteen which deal with Mercian affairs and twelve concerned with northern and Scottish affairs.[9] So these manuscripts of the *Chronicle* can be summarized as C being pro-Mercian, E being pro-Godwin and D pursuing a more neutral agenda, related to the royal court. They illustrate the fault-lines that threatened the English establishment in the years preceding 1066. Cnut had helped create this political earthquake zone through his promotion of Godwin and Leofric.

These competing views mean that the final decades of Anglo-Saxon history have to be followed through the writings of annalists whose 'political prejudices were partly a function of the very politics they describe'.[10] The rival earls were not only competing against each other, but were also causing factionalism among the wider population, as reflected in the monastic communities producing the *Chronicle*. This weakened the late Anglo-Saxon political system, and under a king made weak through

Viking-induced exile (Edward the Confessor) these weaknesses would increase in the decades leading up to the Norman Conquest (*see* Chapter 8). Indeed, these developments, which were rooted in Cnut's strategies of rule, would help to cause the Norman Conquest and all that followed from it.

Cnut in Scandinavia

As we have already seen in Chapter 3, despite being the King of Denmark, Cnut spent very little time in the country and only visited Denmark six times between 1016 and 1035. Despite this, the military support he was able to muster for his campaigns against Norway shows that he still had significant power there.[11] What is clear, though, is that Cnut was an Anglophile. Despite his Scandinavian origins and his military conquest of England, it was England, not Scandinavia, that was uppermost in his mind. Given the relative wealth of the two countries, this should not come as a surprise: England was the greater prize.

Following Cnut's visit to Scandinavia in 1023, the next major incident with regard to international relations in Scandinavia was the Battle of Holy River in 1026. This battle resulted from a joint enterprise by the kings of Norway and Sweden, who felt threatened by the influence of Cnut.[12] It may also have involved Earl Úlf in his capacity as regent of Denmark. According to the thirteenth-century Icelandic historian Snorri Sturluson, in his book *Heimskringla* (*Circle of the World*) – his compilation of sagas about the kings of Norway – Úlf spearheaded a plot to put Cnut's son, Harthacnut, on the throne of Denmark, although there is no other evidence to support this assertion. The late-twelfth/early-thirteenth-century Danish historian Saxo Grammaticus and manuscript *E* of the *Chronicle* do, however, place Úlf and his brother Eglaf on the opposing side to Cnut at the Battle of Holy River.

The outcome of this battle is contentious, with Cnut claiming victory in a letter to the English and contemporary poetic evidence also being cited as evidence that Cnut was victorious. However, the *Chronicle* maintains that it was his enemies who held possession of the battlefield. One thing that is clear is that Úlf was killed; Saxo Grammaticus alleges that Úlf was assassinated in the church at Roskilde.[13] Although the outcome of the Battle of Holy River is disputed, it left the opponents of Cnut still able to negotiate a peace treaty, indicating that they remained sufficiently strong enough to resist a settlement imposed by Cnut. On the other hand, Cnut was able to travel immediately to Rome, so his opponents were clearly also not strong enough to take advantage of his absence.[14]

In Cnut's letter home to England, after the Battle of Holy River, he claimed to be king of all England, Denmark, of the Norwegians and some of the Swedes. If this is true, it means he had already seized the crown of Norway. John of Worcester – a twelfth-century English chronicler – asserted that Cnut heard that the Norwegian nobles were discontented and, in response, sent them gold and silver in order to secure their future support for an expansion of his rule into Norway.[15] However, it seems likely – given that Olaf Haraldsson remained on the Norwegian throne until 1028 – that this claim by Cnut of rule over Norway in 1026 does not have a firm foundation.

The significance of the Swedish claim in Cnut's letter is obscure. It cannot have been a hereditary claim based on Svein Forkbeard's overlordship over the King of Sweden, since other evidence reveals the continued existence of a King of the Svear, the main tribal group in Sweden, despite Cnut's claim. Instead, the Sueones over whom Cnut claimed to be king were probably simply those who had served in his army.[16] There is a small group of coins struck in Sigtuna in Sweden that may be relevant in this discussion. These carry the legend *CNVT REX SW* (*Cnut rex Swevorum*) but, since they all were struck by the same coin-die, it is more likely that it was simply an adaptation of a coin of Cnut already in existence and used in a restricted geographical area. This seems more likely than the alternative interpretation that Cnut was king over all the Svear of Sweden,[17] and indicates that, although Cnut was by far the most dominant of the three rival Scandinavian kings, even after the Battle of Holy River he still did not exercise any substantial political power over the other two kingdoms. Both Norway and Sweden at this point retained their independent dynasties, even if Cnut operated as an overlord.

Despite this, Cnut returned to Scandinavia again in 1028 to reassert his authority over the Norwegians. The C manuscript of the *Chronicle* says that in 1028 Cnut sailed for Norway and Olaf Haraldsson of Norway was unable to mount any effective resistance. Olaf's position had already been weakened by a pagan backlash against his firm, Christian-oriented rule. Cnut undermined this further through generous bribes to Norwegian nobles and promises of greater freedom: he was eventually accepted by the Norwegian nobles, and consolidated his control when he appointed Earl Hakon of Lade as his governor. The earls of Lade were powerful and semi-independent rulers of their part of Norway and had, at various points in Norway's history, taken control of the kingdom as a whole.

Hakon died in 1030 and this gave Olaf Haraldsson the opportunity to try to regain his throne, and he returned to Norway. However, he was killed at the Battle of Stiklestad, near Trondheim, by his own people. Also present at the battle was his half-brother Harald Sigurdsson, better known as Harald Hardrada, who would later become King of Norway and play a pivotal role in the events of 1066. This gave Cnut the opportunity to provide an inheritance for his son Svein Cnutsson – his son by his English wife/mistress, Ælfgifu of Northampton – who was named King of Norway.[18]

The empire of Cnut was, in part, a recreation of the overlordships established by both his father and his grandfather. Cnut inherited an alliance with Sweden, but control of Norway was lost to Olaf Haraldsson. This meant that it took him time to recreate his father's empire and it was not until 1028 that he was in the position that his father had been in, in 1013. This, however, does not deny his achievements, which were based upon political, military, administrative and diplomatic skills.[19] This is made particularly impressive by the fact that he was in England, not Scandinavia, for most of this period.

Unfortunately, nothing is straightforward and the reign of Svein Cnutsson and his mother, Ælfgifu, was to prove to be a failure once the Norwegians realized that they had merely swapped the firm hand of Olaf Haraldsson for an even harsher, foreign master. Svein and Ælfgifu tried to exert greater control over the Norwegian people in terms of taxation and punishment, which led to widespread resentment. This resentment was combined with the growing cult of King or 'Saint' Olaf Haraldsson, and led to the deterioration of the Danish position in Norway and eventually to it being overthrown in 1034.[20] This meant that, by the end of Cnut's reign, he had even less power in Norway than he had enjoyed at the beginning of his time as king: by forcing a Danish ruler onto the Norwegian population, Cnut may have demonstrated that he exercised the political authority in Norway, but in so doing he also alienated the Norwegian people. They then reacted against this control, and ultimately Svein Cnutsson and Ælfgifu of Northampton were forced out of Norway. The Emperor of the North had overplayed his hand.

The rise of the cult of Olaf Haraldsson has usually been seen as one of the main indications of the unpopularity of Svein and Ælfgifu. Despite his having been deposed by his own people, Olaf's cult grew rapidly after his death and he is, to this day, the patron saint of Norway. It should come as no surprise that the rise of the cult of St Olaf should coincide with Norway being under foreign domination and that this should become a focal point for both popular dissatisfaction and also for political wrangling on behalf of the elites.[21] The new situation clearly caused many Norwegians to revise their memories of life under Olaf.

One of the best sources of evidence for the early growth of this cult is in the poem *Glælognskviða* (*Sea-Calm Poem*) which is the oldest evidence of the sanctity of Olaf. It was composed by the Icelandic poet Thórarinn Loftunga, who seems to have been the court poet for Svein Cnutsson. In the poem Thórarinn appears to be urging Svein to support the cult of Olaf in order to defuse this incendiary focus for anti-Danish feeling in Norway.[22] The poet suggests that by allying himself with the cult of Olaf, Svein may be able to present himself as a legitimate heir rather than a foreign occupying force. This implies that control of Olaf's cult could become a powerful political tool and could function as a means of reconciliation between the people of Norway and their Danish king.[23] This can be seen in much the same way as Cnut's veneration of Anglo-Saxon saints, including Edward King and Martyr (*see* later in this chapter), and the later veneration of Edward the Confessor under Norman rule.

Cnut and foreign affairs outside Scandinavia

Following his successes in Scandinavia in 1030, Cnut apparently took the opportunity to travel even further away from home, to the Holy See in Rome. Very little is known about this visit and it may be simply a scribal error on the part of the chroniclers, as Cnut was definitely in Rome in 1027, when he attended the coronation of the Holy Roman Emperor Conrad II. If he did visit again in 1030, then it was an additional journey in a very busy year.

The year 1030 seems to have been a busy one for Cnut. The *Chronicle* states that he went to Scotland and there received the submission of three kings: Malcolm II, Mælbæth and Iehmarc. Malcolm II was the king of Scotland from 1005 to his death in 1034. He is referred to in the *Irish Annals* as *ard rí Alban* (high king of Scotland) and, as with the Irish 'high kings', Malcolm was likely one of several kings within the geographic region of modern-day Scotland. It has been suggested that Mælbæth is Shakespeare's Macbeth, who later deposed Malcolm II's grandson, Duncan, in 1040. Iehmarc is commonly considered to be Echmarcach mac Ragnaill, who was recorded on his death as being 'King of the Rhinns'. This was part of Galloway, but at the height of his power he was also the King of Dublin and ruler of the Isle of Man – a loose empire encompassing the areas of Norse influence in the Irish Sea region.

It is unclear exactly what precipitated these three kings' submission to Cnut; what is clear, however, is that this shows a king who was dominant and in control of mainland Britain.

The *Encomium* lists among Cnut's dominions not only England, Denmark and Norway but also *Brittania* and *Scottia*. The latter may well be a reference to the submission of the three Scottish kings, but the reference to *Brittania* (the Welsh) is a little harder to pin down. The West Saxon royal house had long had a complex history with the Welsh, with earlier Anglo-Saxon kings, such as Athelstan and Edgar, nominally at least being the overlords of the Welsh princes. There are records from Æthelstan's reign of Welsh princes witnessing his charters and when Edgar was crowned at Bath, in 973, he was portrayed as King of the Britons. The evidence for Cnut's power in Wales comes from a forged twelfth-century charter from Llandaff. This charter purports to show that Rhydderch ab Iestyn, King of Gwent and Morgannwy and later ruler of the kingdom of Deuheubarth, confirmed the appointment of the Bishop of Llandaff with the support of the archbishop of Canterbury and letters from Cnut. Although not an accurate document, this shows that the forger assumed that it was reasonable to portray Cnut as intervening in Wales. In support of this view is the fact that Rhydderch's son was killed by the English in 1035, although the circumstances surrounding his death are entirely unknown. Whatever the truth of the claims of the *Encomium*, they clearly show the author trying to place Cnut among the greatest of the kings of Anglo-Saxon England.

Cnut was not just successful in the British Isles since, like the greatest Anglo-Saxon king before him, Athelstan, he also dabbled in the affairs of the continent. Cnut's kingdom of Denmark bordered Germany, and the Danes had a long and difficult history with the Germans. However, when Cnut attended the coronation of the Emperor Conrad in Rome, he did so with pride, as recorded in his letter of that year written to his followers in England. This friendly relationship led to the betrothal of Cnut's daughter, Gunnhild, to Conrad's heir, Henry, in 1034 and they were married in 1036. Though Gunnhild died two years later, the alliance is testament to the attractiveness of an alliance with Cnut; although it perhaps says more about him as King of Denmark than King of England, given the German campaigns against the Poles in the early 1030s. As king of Denmark, Cnut was a useful ally for the Emperor: friendship with Denmark allowed the ruler of Germany the opportunity to deal with his eastern neighbours without fear of interference from his western one.

The relationship with Normandy was also important, as highlighted by the marriage between Cnut and Emma, widow of King Æthelred II and sister of the Duke of Normandy. Following the death of Emma's brother Richard, Cnut arranged the marriage of his sister Estrith to the new Duke of Normandy, Robert. The fact that Cnut felt this match was necessary shows that he must have been concerned that Robert would support his nephews – Emma and Æthelred II's sons, the æthelings Edward and Alfred – in an attempt to regain their father's throne. This complex set of moves was part of the political game involving England and Normandy that had been set in motion by the Viking Wars and which was accelerated by Cnut's Viking Conquest of England.

Cnut and the English Church

One area of Cnut's reign about which a lot is known is his relationship with the English Church. Cnut was undoubtedly a Christian when he became King of England in 1016. However, Danish Christianity only went back as far as Cnut's grandfather, Harald Bluetooth, and so Cnut was not in a position to place Danish churchmen in places of prominence in England, as he had done with secular appointments.

Along with many other kings and nobles of the period, Cnut was a generous patron to the Church. One of the most enduring images of this can be found in the *Liber Vitae* (*Book of Life*), a manuscript in the New Minster, Winchester, which contains a drawing showing Cnut and Emma donating a cross to the Minster. This was not the only religious institution to which Cnut made donations: he is also recorded as bestowing valuable gifts of gold and silver on Abingdon, Westminster Abbey and Wilton. Cnut also made generous gifts of land to numerous religious houses across England, from Durham in the north to St German's in Cornwall in the south. Cnut's letter from 1027 describes his visit to Rome of that year and reports how he went to Rome to ask forgiveness of his sins and the safety of his subjects, as well as the fact that he had negotiated with the pope a reduction in the fees English archbishops had to pay when they went to Rome to collect their *pallium*, the woollen liturgical vestment that was conferred on an archbishop by the pope. Cnut was clearly displaying his credentials as a Christian monarch.

One way in which Cnut combined his Anglophile tendencies with his Christian piety was in the veneration of Anglo-Saxon saints, including Edward King and Martyr. Edward had been king between 975 and 978; he was an unremarkable monarch – partly due to the short length of his reign – but on 18 March 978 he was murdered by persons unknown while visiting his stepmother at Corfe in Dorset. The events surrounding his murder are very unclear, and despite his exalted position as King of England no culprits were ever identified and no one was brought to account for his murder.

The feast of Edward King and Martyr was referred to in all the surviving manuscripts of a lawcode known as *I Cnut*, a lawcode from 1018 that is believed to have been written by Wulfstan, Archbishop of York. The benefits that could be gained through relationship to a royal saint may explain why Cnut chose to include the references to the feast day of Edward King and Martyr within *I Cnut*: he clearly felt that associating his rule with that of his saintly predecessor would increase his prestige.[24]

In addition, in light of the fact that Cnut was not a member of the House of Wessex and had no blood right to the throne, it is likely that he was seeking to legitimize his rule in any way possible, and that the cult of Edward King and Martyr – which was also associated with his predecessor Æthelred II – was one way of doing this. Since there is no evidence that Æthelred II was blamed for Edward's death during this period, this seems more likely than the idea that Cnut was attempting to sully the reputation of Æthelred. In later years the murder was blamed on Æthelred's mother – Edward's stepmother – who it was claimed had masterminded it in order to secure the throne for her son, and this cast a shadow on Æthelred. But there is no evidence that Cnut was motivated to do this.

What all this demonstrates is not just Cnut's piety but also how useful religion was as a political tool. It is likely, given the still very recent conversion of Denmark to Christianity, that Cnut felt the need to demonstrate his faith in order to counteract any doubts about his sincerity as a Christian, the reputation of Vikings as pagan marauders being well established in Anglo-Saxon literature. This generosity toward the English Church and patronage of Anglo-Saxon saints were ways both to visibly show Cnut's faith and also to demonstrate his integration into English society.

Cnut in England: the final years

There is surprisingly little known about Cnut's final five years in England. His movements are uncertain, although it is possible that he visited Glastonbury in November 1032. There are five charters from 1033, which are the most that survive from a single year in his reign. Perhaps the most interesting of the charters from the later part of Cnut's reign is the one called S 975 from 1035, granting land to the monks of Sherborne. This calls on the monks to pray for Cnut's soul, which may indicate that he was already dying when this charter was written. Cnut died on 12 November 1035 and was buried at the Old Minster in Winchester; he was forty-five years old. Today his bones are jumbled with those of other royals in chests kept in Winchester Cathedral, the confusion being the result of Parliamentary looting of the cathedral in 1642, during the English Civil Wars. In time, Cnut's remains may be identified by comparison with mitochondrial DNA from the teeth of the later Danish king, Svein Estrithson (Cnut's nephew), which was recovered by Danish scientists from his burial in Roskilde church in Denmark.[25]

Although he had a fairly long reign, compared with many early medieval monarchs, Cnut still undoubtedly died young and it is to be wondered what more he could have achieved if he had lived longer. Cnut succeeded in holding together a conquered kingdom, he created a top tier of elites who were completely loyal to him, and he may have been recognized as the overlord of the Welsh and Scots. He combined this position of dominance with a role in Scandinavia that at times saw him rule as King of Denmark, overlord of Norway and with influence in Sweden. He married a female relative to the heir to the German emperor and went to Rome at least once – and possibly twice. However, as with many early medieval monarchs, his power and control was bound up with him as an individual and his hard-won empire was to disintegrate soon after his death: despite the seeming stability of his rule, Cnut's death precipitated a succession crisis as his sons fought bitterly over the crown. Within seven years of Cnut's death the royal Anglo-Saxon line of Cerdic would once again be on the throne of England.

The impact of the rule of Cnut should not be seen solely in terms of how long Danish monarchs sat on the English throne. If this was so, the re-establishment of the Anglo-Saxon royal line in 1042 would render it just a passing episode. In reality, the impact of Viking rule was far greater than this: the ramifications of the Danish conquest of England in 1016 would be felt long after the death of Cnut in 1035 and the death of his last surviving son a mere seven years later, in 1042.

CHAPTER 5

Home Thoughts from Abroad: A Postcard from Normandy

Given the trauma of what happened in October 1066 and the Norman Conquest that followed, it is very common today to view this as a national calamity. England was conquered and subjugated by a foreign power. That it was the last time England experienced this makes the matter all the more shocking and significant. After the traumatic events of 1066, England withstood all further attempts at conquest, by Napoleon in 1803–05 and Hitler in 1940. Other invasions, such as that of Prince Louis of France in 1216 or the French invasion of Ireland in 1796, were either side-shows in the case of the latter or failed to achieve their goal despite early success in the case of the former. This only further emphasizes the significance of 1066. That so many of these invasion plans had their origins in France makes the defeat in 1066 all the more shocking. Hundreds of years of rivalry between England and its closest continental neighbour can make the 'French victory' of 1066 a very bitter pill to swallow. It is often presented in popular historical accounts as a clearly demarcated national dispute with the English on one side and the Normans (French in disguise) on the other. And this time the Normans (French) won. It was a humiliation that would not be allowed to happen again over the next millennium.

England and her European neighbours

Given this mental construct of events, it is tempting to see all Norman involvement in late Anglo-Saxon England as unwanted, unwarranted and unwelcome. They were 'over-foreign, over-confident and over-here' to parody some English attitudes towards American GIs in World War Two. And what is worse (in contrast to those GIs, whose involvement in the war was actually desperately needed) these Norman interlopers were not only unwanted but actually ended up being on the winning side. Galling beyond belief! English patriotism is certainly affronted and a millennium of getting used to it has not helped take the edge off the sting of defeat. The matter only gets worse when one reflects that it was an English ruler – Edward the Confessor – who apparently opened the door to these intruders and then did all he could to wedge it open in the face of patriotic opposition by the Godwin family and their allies (*see* Chapter 8). Edward's motivation becomes difficult to understand, his apparent betrayal of English national interests seems shocking, and the consequences of his actions were traumatic.

All of the above, though stated in a rather extreme form, will not sound unfamiliar to English readers; most think it or something like it. But it is anachronistic and does not do justice to the actual events of the eleventh century. To be fair, it is not *entirely* unjustified and, as we shall see (in Chapters 8 and 9), there was a significant amount of opposition to the Norman (and French) involvement in English Church and state in the 1050s, and the resistance to the Norman invasion in 1066 was real and clearly had widespread support. But it is wrong to regard everyone from beyond the English Channel as representing unwanted intrusions into Anglo-Saxon society. Indeed, the Anglo-Saxons were themselves 'intruders' (without getting into the debate about the nature of the early Anglo-Saxon invasions and settlement) and had ancestral and ongoing connections beyond the sea.

In addition, via the Christian Church non-English people had played a vital role within Anglo-Saxon society from the seventh century onwards. The Anglo-Saxon Church was part of a Europe-wide community and the ethnic make-up of its leadership reflected this. Clerics and their skills were employed from across Western Europe and beyond. Alfred the Great, for example, had pulled in assistance with his educational programme from other areas of England (outside of his native Wessex), from Wales and from Francia (which broadly comprised France, Belgium and western Germany). Anglo-Saxon England did not exist in some kind of insular 'bubble'; England never has. Foreign marriage alliances and negotiations had preoccupied the politics of Offa of Mercia in the eighth century, of Alfred the Great's father Æthelwulf in the ninth century and his royal successors in the tenth century. 'Abroad' was not alien, although it was not always friendly, either.

What this means is that when rulers of England, from Æthelred II to Edward the Confessor, sought foreign alliances they were not acting without historical precedent and neither were they necessarily acting against the national interest. On the contrary, it was crucial to have understandings and alliances with neighbouring polities, and in an age when these were cemented by royal marriages this inevitably created a web of connections, expectations and dynastic implications. It was in such a world that Anglo-Saxon elites could come to terms with 'foreign rulers' such as Svein Forkbeard and Cnut. And could then get caught up in the dynastic politics of Denmark and Norway as a consequence.

Even as late as 1216, the invitation extended by the rebellious barons to

Prince Louis of France to assist them meant that for barons fearing defeat at the hands of King John or during the uncertain imminent minority of his son, 'the prospect of a foreign Prince, in all likelihood ruling from a distance in Paris, was a preferable option.'[1] In such a world there was nothing unusual or unpatriotic in a close alliance with Normandy in the eleventh century. Indeed, an alliance with a potentially useful ally (or potentially troubling enemy) just across the English Channel was both understandable and responsible, and constituted an important piece within the jigsaw of Anglo-Saxon diplomacy during the extended Viking Wars. That it might create future dynastic expectations was par for the course. That it might lead to violent conquest could not have been antici-pated. History is lived forwards, not backwards. And the trouble with hindsight is that it colours the actions of the past with the outlook and awareness of the present; as if those in the past should somehow have been able to predict the unpredictable, and view their 'current' events with the benefit of hindsight.

This should make us less sensitive to the presence of Normans and other Frenchmen in the dynastic connections and court politics of the eleventh century: we need to avoid the anachronisms of later national competitiveness. In addition, we have to suspend our knowledge of the events of 1066 when assessing these earlier involvements, which were intimately connected with the events of the Viking Wars. But first we need to establish just who were these Normans who were to become so important in deciding the trajectory of English history.

Who were the Normans?

By the mid-eleventh century the Normans were second- or third-gener-ation immigrants to northern France from Scandinavia. Their origins lay in the same waves of Viking raiders and settlers that had impacted on Anglo-Saxon England and which had led to widespread land seizure there in the late ninth and early tenth centuries.

Like the Vikings in England, the Normans had their own traditions of heroic ancestors who had carved out new lands far from their Scan-dinavian homelands. The foundation myth of Normandy maintained that the land of Normandy ('land of the northmen') had originally been granted to their founder, Rollo (or Rolf), in about 911 by the Frankish king Charles III. Rollo was probably a Norwegian who led a force that was mostly Danish.[2] Prior to this, he had taken part in the Viking siege of Paris in 886, but had finally been defeated and this was then followed by an attempt to prevent him causing further trouble: it was this that led to the 911 land grant. As a consequence, Rollo and his successors ruled their new territory as frontier or 'marcher' lords on behalf of the Frankish king. As a consequence of this the Norman system of rule was influenced by Frankish practices, just as Scandinavians in England were greatly influenced by Anglo-Saxon customs, while also making their own contributions to a new and hybrid society. The name of the newcomers – French *Normands* and Latin *Nortmanni* – reflected their Viking ancestry.

The boundaries of the land granted to these 'northmen' were established by the treaty of Saint-Clair-sur-Epte, which was agreed between King Charles III of West Francia and the Viking chieftain Rollo referred to earlier. It lay within the former Frankish sub-kingdom of Neustria; Rollo and his followers gained land between the river Epte and the Atlantic coast, in exchange for their protection against further Viking raids. It was a policy of encouraging a poacher to become a gamekeeper. The area granted to them was roughly equivalent to the northern part of what today is described as Upper Normandy, as far as the river Seine, but was soon extended west of this river boundary; later sources maintained that this was the result of a *foedus*, a formal treaty. In much the same way, Alfred the Great of Wessex had entered into treaty arrangements with Viking invaders in the late ninth century as a way of normalizing relations with these turbulent newcomers through diplomatic obligations, establishing mutually recognized spheres of influence, and attempting to persuade them not to attack his core territories in the future.

Although initially pagan, the new Norse-speaking overlords soon adopted Christianity and Rollo took the name Robert at his baptism. In time the Normans became enthusiastic supporters of the latest papal and Church trends, something that would earn Duke William of Normandy a papal banner in 1066 and a commission to reform aspects of the Anglo-Saxon Church. In addition, Norse speech soon gave way to a form of French that survives today as 'Norman' (*Nourmaund*), a regional form of French. The form of language they used in the eleventh century is often described today as 'Norman-French'. Some of its vocabulary reflected its Norse roots in Scandinavia and this may have influenced some aspects of pronunciation, too.

The rulers of Normandy were not kings but dukes. The title they originally carried was that of 'count', from the Latin *comes*, and Rollo was formally styled the 'count of Rouen'. However, Rollo/Robert's great-grandson Richard II (duke from 996 to 1026) adopted the title 'duke', derived from the Latin *dux*. From then onwards we can talk of dukes of Normandy. Richard II's grandson was Duke William (duke from 1035 to 1087).

The position of Rollo was assisted by the fact that his achievement coincided with a period of weaker kingship in the Western Frankish kingdom. This meant that there was little Frankish interference in the area around Rouen or further west, as Rollo (who lived until 927) settled into his new role and established his power base.

Within Normandy the military power of the duke rested on his relationship with the great landowners under his control. In the Latin terms that soon became adopted to describe these relationships, these local lords were his *fidelis* (his faithful men) and the duke was the *dominus* (the overall lord). It was this *familia* (a group bound by ties of family and loyalty) that governed Normandy and whose members owed personal loyalty to the duke. There were clear parallels to these kinds of relationship in Anglo-Saxon England too, but there were differences also.

In contrast to Anglo-Saxon England, government in Normandy was less sophisticated and less centralized. For example, instead of the efficient Anglo-Saxon system of regular re-coinage, and despite the fact that Norman dukes controlled the coinage in Normandy, when William became duke in 1035 no new coins had been minted there since the time of his grandfather, Richard II. This made Anglo-Saxon England – with its efficient coinage and taxation, and its system of royal government with its writs, shire courts and sheriffs doing the king's bidding – a very attractive proposition. It was a rich and desirable prize, not that it would be viewed in these terms in Normandy until the late 1050s. Duke William (duke from 1035) later played a major part in tightening control by government over the local elites and in bringing them more fully under ducal control. This would greatly assist his preparations to invade England in 1066, but that is getting ahead of our story.

Returning to Normandy, while the sophistication of its government might have lagged behind that of England, it was still more orderly than many neighbouring French regions. In Normandy structures of government that had collapsed elsewhere in France were either preserved or revived. A titled aristocracy (counts) had been established below the position of the duke; viscounts administered royal estates; continued holding of these positions was dependent on the duke; warfare was directed outside of the duchy; and within it there was not the proliferation of castles and endemic warfare found in other parts of France.[3]

Nevertheless, in terms of warfare, the less centralized (and sometimes anarchic) nature of Normandy had led to local nobles developing defended residences that we would recognize as early castles. Defended residences existed in Anglo-Saxon England too, but not to the same extent as in Normandy and this was why the Norman Conquest, when it eventually occurred, brought a rash of castles across England that was innovative as well as intimidating. It is traditional to describe these early Norman castles (both in Normandy and in England) as 'motte and bailey' castles. In the usual descriptions these consist of a wooden stockade around an area containing living quarters and stabling (the 'bailey') with a defended tower on top of a mound of earth (the 'motte') into which defenders could retreat if the bailey's defences were breached. Around the stockade a ditch or moat (dry or water-filled) would be dug. In reality, very few early castles in Normandy and in England fall into this category. Most, in fact, were simple defended ring-works (much like a Wild West fort) and the motte and bailey variant seems to have been a slightly later development, prior to the construction of ever-more elaborate defences built of stone.

Associated with the Norman use of castles was the development of mounted warfare involving knights. These formed a mounted military elite that was focused on preparing for and carrying out warfare; this was a development that occurred in the century after Rollo's establishment of the duchy. Grants of land gave knights the resources with which they could fund their military expenditure. The duke and the great landowners had their own groups of dependent knights who owed them loyalty in return for grants of land: in times of war the duke call up his household knights and summoned his barons to call up theirs, 'baron' being the term used to describe those landowners who held their estates directly from the duke (and later the king).

In contrast, Anglo-Saxon warriors might ride to battle but still fought on foot in the traditional Germanic and Scandinavian fashion. The Anglo-Saxon king could call on his own household warriors (often called 'huscarls', in the Danish fashion, by the 1020s) and those of the great earls, but he also relied on a general levy of local landowners, the 'thegns', who made up the 'fyrd' (or local call-up). The fyrd could put on an impressive fighting performance, as would be seen in the three great battles of 1066 (*see* Chapter 9), but it was the Normans, with their knights, who were at the cutting edge of eleventh-century military technology. And this would have its effect on 14 October 1066.

Most Norman knights in the early eleventh century, although skilled militarily, were relatively poor and land-hungry. As a result, by 1066 Normandy had been exporting fighting horsemen for over forty years, adventurers who sought payment as mercenaries in other parts of Europe and became involved in the conflicts in these areas. In this way Norman-derived influence and culture became an influential force over a wide area. By 1016 at the latest, Norman knights were fighting and settling in southern Italy, from where they later wrested Sicily from Islamic control. Some fought against the Byzantine Empire, while others fought for it; these last fought as far from home as Armenia and Georgia.

So, how Scandinavian were the Normans of Normandy by the early eleventh century? On one hand they had become very French. On the Bayeux Tapestry (really an embroidery) they are referred to as the 'Franci'.[4] Their language, as we have seen, had become basically French with Scandinavian influences: they were now speaking a 'Romance' language not a 'North Germanic' one. Their methods of fighting had evolved away from the more traditional forms still practised in Anglo-Saxon England

and in Scandinavia. The combined evidence of place-names, personal names, and language suggests relatively small numbers of Scandinavian settlers in the area, who soon intermarried with the local Frankish families. By the mid-tenth century there were few Norse speakers in Rouen,[5] although in Bayeux they could be recognized for a further generation.[6] It is noteworthy that no objects carrying runes have so far been discovered in Normandy, which indicates that Norse culture there rapidly declined and settlers became assimilated to local customs and language.[7]

Nevertheless, despite their adoption of Frankish characteristics, the Normans remained conscious of their northern roots and remained 'participants in the maritime culture of the world of the northern seas'.[8] It is revealing that the few Norse words that were borrowed by the French language refer to ships and shipping. They were distinct from their French neighbours and constituted a recognizable and hybrid culture, although one heavily indebted to the French. They had not shaken off their Viking-ness, even if they had greatly modified it, which was apparent in the way they still dabbled in the politics of Scandinavia as it affected England. When Viking fleets troubled England in the year 1000, it was to Normandy that they went afterwards. When Duke Robert I considered invading England (as we shall shortly see) and Duke William successfully did so, they were drawing on maritime and military traditions that arose from their Viking past. Indeed, Duke Robert was apparently explicitly reminded of this when considering an English adventure.

What role did the Normans play in the foreign policy of England up to 1016?

Since the Normans occupied the key Channel ports facing England, it became a key part of English foreign policy to neutralize the potential threat of Viking raiding armies using such bases as jumping-off points for attacks on England. They could also provide safe havens for Viking fleets driven from English shores as they regrouped for further attacks. As Scandinavian attacks accelerated again from the 990s, the position of Normandy became extremely important.

In 991 the Norman Duke Richard I (duke from 942 to 996) entered into a diplomatic alliance with Æthelred II of England.[9] So great had become the enmity between England and Normandy that 'it required a papal envoy to resolve it and to make a treaty'.[10] The alliance, though, does not seem to have long outlived the duke since in the year 1000, according to the *Anglo-Saxon Chronicle*, 'the enemy fleet had gone to Richard's kingdom that summer.'[11] 'Richard' is Duke Richard II of Normandy (duke from 996 to 1026) and the description of his dukedom as a 'kingdom' is a mistake. In the year 1000 Richard II had been duke for just four years and was clearly still keeping his options open with regard to alliances. It looks as if the alliance of 991 with England had lapsed, or perhaps that Richard II was playing both sides: Anglo-Saxons and Scandinavian raiders. Certainly the English clearly considered he had become dangerous as, in response, they launched an – unsuccessful – raid on the Cotentin Peninsula. It seems obvious that this was a punishment for harbouring (quite literally) a Viking fleet the previous summer.

Neither side seems to have been happy with this ongoing state of hostilities as the new millennium began, and what followed was a decisive move to get things back to the happier situation of 991, only this time the alliance would be stronger. In 1002 Æthelred II married Emma of Normandy, sister of Duke Richard II, the intention being to 'draw the duke away from his Scandinavian allies.'[12] The result was far from perfect since Viking fleets continued to seek shelter in Normandy,[13] but at least it limited the problem posed by Normandy.

The later Norman historian William of Jumièges, writing shortly before 1060 in his chronicle entitled *Gesta Normannorum Ducum* (*Deeds of the Norman Dukes*), suggests that the raid on the Cotentin occurred *after* the marriage of Æthelred II to Emma.[14] This seems difficult to reconcile with the rapprochement between England and Normandy that the marriage symbolized, so perhaps the English naval raid predated it or even accompanied it as an incentive to the Normans to agree to the alliance it represented. On the other hand, William may have been correct, which would suggest that it took a while for the alliance to really bed in. Or, maybe, Duke Richard continued to play both sides for a time after his sister's marriage and the English raid was designed to put an end to this duplicity.

This marriage bound England and Normandy together in a dynastic alliance that would last until the death of Cnut in 1035 and beyond, since as we saw in Chapter 3, Cnut married Emma following the death of Æthelred II and his own taking of the throne when Edmund Ironside died. Even if the alliance did not prevent the fugitive children of Æthelred II from being given shelter in Normandy after 1016, it still succeeded in neutralizing Normandy as a source of really serious trouble for Cnut as he sought to rule both England and Denmark. On Cnut's death it would be a platform for an abortive attempt by these two exiled sons to return to England (as we shall see in Chapter 6) and Normandy would then continue to shelter the surviving son of Æthelred until 1041, but its challenge did not extend much beyond this. In short: the Anglo-Norman understanding held up fairly well for forty years.

From Æthelred II's marriage to Emma came three children: the ætheling Edward (later called the Confessor) who would later rule as King of England; the ætheling Alfred, who would die at the hands of Godwin and Harald Harefoot in 1036 as we shall see in Chapter 6; and Godgifu, who was first married to Drogo of Mantes, Count of Vexin, and then to

Eustace II, who was Count of Boulogne. Like Æthelred II's marriage to Emma of Normandy, these two marriages were designed to strengthen diplomatic relations with key players on the other side of the English Channel.

This strengthening of the alliance with Normandy meant that Æthelred II had a place of refuge in 1013 when Svein Forkbeard invaded England (see Chapter 2). Æthelred fled to Normandy with his family (although Emma travelled separately from her husband and children), but he briefly returned as king after Svein died suddenly in 1014; Æthelred II himself died in 1016. Though short-lived for Æthelred, this Norman exile was a pointer to things to come for his sons by Emma.

The exile of the æthelings Edward and Alfred in Normandy

Ætheling Edward (the future 'Confessor') returned into exile in Normandy and rejoined his brother, Alfred, in 1016 when Cnut took the throne of England following the death of Edmund Ironside (*see* Chapter 2). For the duration of Cnut's reign (1016–35) it was too dangerous to return, and Edward would be in exile in Normandy until 1041. How he felt about his mother, Emma, returning to England in July 1017 to marry Cnut we can only speculate; it certainly did not bode well for his chances of ever succeeding to the English throne. He and his brother may well have felt abandoned in Normandy. Cnut may have felt that, though they were out of his reach, the presence of their mother at his court offered him at least some control over their behaviour.[15]

What is clear is that Edward and Alfred were relatively safe in Normandy, but politically out in the cold. There is no evidence that their uncle, Emma's brother Duke Richard II, made any effort to support an armed invasion to reinstate them in England prior to his own death in 1026. They would not be returned by a Norman military intervention while he was duke, that seems clear. Edward's negative behaviour towards his mother once he became king in 1042 suggests that there was a legacy of bitterness and resentment towards her: it may well have dated from 1017 and the sense of desperation that he must have felt particularly acutely in the 1020s.

We know little of the details of the exile of the two royal brothers. Given that their sister, Godgifu, was married to Drogo of Mantes we may assume that some assistance was forthcoming from that quarter, but this is speculation. What we do know is that by the early 1030s Edward was in Normandy (assuming he had ever left it). At that time he witnessed four charters there and in two of them he described himself as 'king of England'. Clearly he had not given up hope.

It is possible that at this time this hope was given a boost by the actions of a new duke in Normandy. Robert I became ruler of Normandy in 1027 (following the short reign of his brother, Duke Richard III, 1026–7), and ruled until 1035 (the same year that Cnut died in England). In the later *Gesta Normannorum Ducum*, William of Jumièges recorded a tradition that Robert I dispatched a naval expedition in support of a bid by Edward for the English throne. The same tradition is also found in another Norman source, the *Carmen de Hastingae Proelio* (*Song of the Battle of Hastings*), an early source for the Norman Conquest and almost certainly written early in 1067. In this source Robert I was urged to emulate his ancestors who had invaded Britain before him (clearly a reference to Viking raids). William of Jumièges adds that bad weather caused the invasion to be aborted and that the fleet was redirected to Brittany.

The corroboration of this tradition suggests that something indeed happened in support of Edward's claim to the throne. If so, this is the only time that Cnut was challenged by a significant Norman commitment to Edward's cause – and it came to nothing. The likelihood of a real invasion attempt is strengthened by the fact that William of Jumièges states that Fécamp was the port from which it sailed and a charter of 1033 shows that Duke Robert I was indeed there that year and was accompanied by both the æthelings, Edward and Alfred. It is around this time that Edward witnessed charters, styling himself as 'king', and this may have been because he had hopes of finally getting the English crown. It is, though, possible that Britain and Brittany were confused in the original tradition and that the whole expedition was actually aimed at Brittany. In which case, this one Norman military intervention on behalf of Edward vanishes. Either way, there was in the event no such Norman invasion of England. Cnut, married to a Norman princess, may have felt that something of the old Norman alliance was still benefiting him and his rule, even if it had become somewhat shaky since 1027 and the accession of Duke Robert I.

Despite this relative inactivity by his Norman hosts on his behalf, Edward was still provided with a safe home and some support and for this, at least, the later evidence of his Norman sympathies suggests that he was grateful. A highly questionable later source – Book II of the *Vita Edwardi Regis* (*Life of King Edward*) written c.1065–7 – states that while in Normandy he had performed miraculous cures of the sick, so great was his sanctity. This has led some later chroniclers and historians to suggest that he lived in a monastic community while in exile and intended to enter the Church. This is highly unlikely for two reasons. Firstly, the motivation of the writer of the *Vita Edwardi Regis* is all too obvious: to promote the idea of King Edward's saintliness following his death in 1066. Secondly, there is more plausible evidence that Edward and his brother were, in reality, brought up as knights within the secular context of the ducal court in Normandy. This is explicitly stated by the Norman monastic writer, William of Jumièges, in the late 1050s and was repeated by the Norman chronicler William of Poitiers in the 1070s.

How well they lived is difficult to reconstruct, and this is a pity as it would be a measure of the extent of their Norman support. William of Poitiers later claimed that they had been accorded great *honores* ('honours') and *beneficia* ('benefits') while in exile in Normandy. However, the Latin terms *honores* and *beneficia* can mean both respect and kindness *and* land and property.[16] Since no Norman writer ever records an actual estate or piece of property given to them, there is a real possibility that they benefited from honourable treatment but not much monetary generosity. This lack of generosity might be explainable by the fact that Duke Richard II was very probably involved in the negotiations that led to his sister marrying Cnut. In this case, this represented a new alliance between Normandy and England,[17] between the Viking king of England and the descendant of Vikings, the Duke of Normandy. Not assisting the exiled sons of Æthelred II, other than providing a safe home for them, may have been part of such a deal.

As we have seen, they witnessed charters while in the ducal household, which gives us something of a fix on where they resided. Edward appears on the witness list of three charters under Duke Robert I (two of these are also witnessed by his brother, Alfred) and one under Duke William. It is interesting to note that their names come fairly low down on the list of witnesses and on one, from April 1033, they are almost at the very bottom of a long list of names; this does not speak well with regard to their status. It seems that, while they were treated respectfully, nobody thought that they had a lot of political value. As a result, not a lot of effort was invested in them!

In reality, the exiled Edward and Alfred may have split their time between a number of foreign courts: relatives occupied positions of power in an arc from Flanders to Brittany. We know Edward was in Bruges at least once, and on his return to England in 1041 he brought with him friends and associates not only from Normandy but also from Mantes, Brittany and Lorraine.

As we shall see in Chapter 6, the situation dramatically changed on the death of Cnut in 1035. In 1036 both exiled æthelings – Alfred and Edward – returned to England. For Alfred it was a disaster that led to his death; for Edward it was little more than an unsuccessful raid with Norman assistance. The later Norman historians, William of Jumièges and William of Poitiers, imply Norman support for his adventure that led to him being resisted and expelled. For those on the receiving end of this attempt, the arrival of Edward and his Norman allies may not have looked much different from the Viking raids they had experienced in the past.

Alfred's return and death is recorded in the *Anglo-Saxon Chronicle*, but we find only Norman records with regard to the separate adventure of Edward – the English sources are silent. That both æthelings were repulsed shows how much they had become isolated from English politics and support by their time spent in Norman exile. The key point at this juncture, though, is that Edward could not have made even this failed attempt without assistance from his Norman hosts. Norman assistance provided to Edward in his failed attempt to return to England indicates increased Norman support for him from the mid-1030s, and put him more firmly in their debt.

Despite this, the situation was not looking good from Edward's perspective. He had failed, his brother was dead and his mother, Emma, had been expelled from England (although she had opted for exile in Flanders rather than Normandy). The game was running in favour of Cnut's sons, Harald Harefoot and Harthacnut, though things could in fact have been better for Harthacnut, far away in Denmark while Harald Harefoot sat on the English throne. In Normandy the new duke William – Edward's first-cousin-once-removed – was only nine years old and had other things on his mind than assisting Edward to take the English throne: simply staying alive was proving to be a challenge for him.

The young William's situation was something of a nightmare. The bastard son of the unmarried Duke Robert I by his mistress Herleva, the man who would one day be known as William 'the Conqueror' was then very much William 'the Bastard'. During his childhood and adolescence rival factions battled to control him and slaughtered each other in order to do so. It was not a happy time. It was not until 1047 that William was able to defeat a rebellion that threatened to destroy him and could finally begin to establish his authority over Normandy. In that year, with assistance from his ally the King of France, he was victorious at the Battle of Val-ès-Dunes, near Caen and crushed his rivals. Getting the upper hand was a challenging process: from 1047 until 1054 William was engaged in almost continuous warfare, and less pressing problems continued until 1060. By that time (and probably sometime in the mid-1050s) he had become a contender for the throne of England, perhaps even the heir (*see* Chapter 8), but that would have seemed highly unlikely in the late 1030s.

When ætheling Edward finally returned to England in 1041 it was largely due to factors within the complicated politics of that country. But Norman sources insist that, in some way, William of Normandy (by then aged thirteen) assisted the return. Whether William of Poitiers had much hard evidence to support this claim is difficult to say, since he did not state much about what it was. He may, in fact, have just been reading back into the events of 1041 the situation of the mid-1050s, augmented by the triumph of 1066 as seen from the standpoint of the late 1070s. However, this may be going *too* far in reducing the extent of Norman support for Edward. William of Poitiers clearly believed that Edward was accompanied by a small escort of Norman knights and other evidence allows us to suggest he came with a small household following, although only one Norman is actually named.

So, to what extent can we regard the returning Edward as 'the Norman candidate for the English throne'?[18] It is difficult to tell and the later – Norman – sources may have exaggerated his reasons for feeling indebted to Normandy and its teenage duke. What we can perhaps say with some confidence is that it was more than he owed to the English establishment, who had been in no rush to aid his return over an exile of twenty-five years. Perhaps the question needs to be re-worded. Given his state of isolation and insecurity when he returned, where might he have considered home to have been (however chilly) and who were his friends (even if not exclusively Norman)? The answer seems fairly obvious. The Norman connection was there and could not be denied.

What were the implications of this Norman connection?

The Norman connection was perhaps the most important foreign connection to be introduced courtesy of the Viking Wars. A direct consequence of Cnut's Viking Conquest was the sending into exile of æthelings Edward and Alfred, both sons of the previous Anglo-Saxon king, Æthelred II. The earlier marriage of Emma of Normandy to Æthelred II (who later married Cnut) had been the first major Norman involvement in the dynastic politics of England; this was deepened by Edward's period of exile there after 1016 and it was this that led to Duke William's dynastic claims and thus to Hastings and 1066.[19]

The experiences of Edward in Normandy clearly greatly affected him. It was inevitable that on his accession to the English throne in 1042 he would be an outsider, but not that he would eventually adopt such a distinctly pro-Norman outlook. As a consequence, the appearance of a Norman-French faction at the court was very much down to Edward himself. This cannot just simply be put down to Edward's being half-Norman; after all, Harthacnut was also half-Norman but was not regarded as particularly pro-Norman. Therefore, Edward's pro-Norman outlook has to have been a result of his growing up in Normandy, an experience that was solely due to the actions of Cnut in 1016. As a direct consequence of this experience, Edward was culturally more Norman-French in terms of habits, preferences and his world-view than would ever had been the case had he grown up in England, whatever his maternal connections.

The English court under King Edward definitely came to eventually have a 'French accent', even if was not specifically Norman (*see* Chapter 8). But, as we shall see, this did not occur immediately and these Normans were not the only foreigners in King Edward's court. There were priests and clerics from Germany (particularly from the area of Lorraine) and the English elites themselves already had well-established links to Flanders, Denmark, Wales and Ireland. To assume that it would eventually be possible to simply divide Edward's court into English and Norman is to take far too simplistic an approach.[20] Chapter 8 will demonstrate that England under Edward the Confessor was more politically complex than this, and at times unstable. Nevertheless, the undeniable reality is that no other previous king of Anglo-Saxon England had had such strong connections with the Normans.

Even if Edward's court (when finally established after 1042) was more cosmopolitan than is sometimes stated, he was the only king who consciously constructed a 'Norman answer' to his 'English problems' and whose death could have (as a consequence) provided the pretext for a Norman invasion. This cannot be denied. We will return to this but, for now, suffice it to say that it was Edward's exile in Normandy that laid the foundations for what was to follow. This was a Viking connection (with Scandinavian-derived Normandy) that was deepened hugely by a Viking cause (the Viking Conquest by Cnut in 1016). Any postcard that Edward the Confessor sent to England from Normandy should have had a picture of a Viking longship on the front!

CHAPTER 6

Sons and Lovers: Cnut's Two Marriages and His Competing Sons

The time in which England formed part of a Viking Anglo-Danish Empire ended with the reigns, in turn between 1035 and 1042, of Cnut's sons from two different marriages: kings Harald Harefoot (also known as Harald I) and Harthacnut. This period of unsettled and disputed succession witnessed the failed return (from Normandy) of the Anglo-Saxon ætheling Alfred (son of Æthelred II), and his mutilation and death. The hatred that this engendered between his surviving brother, ætheling Edward (later to reign as King Edward the Confessor), and Godwin of Wessex would have far-reaching repercussions. Far from being a mere footnote to the more famous reign of Cnut, the events of this period would mean that in 1066 the Viking rulers of both Denmark and Norway thought that they had a claim to the English throne, in addition to the claim of William of Normandy.

The succession crisis

Cnut's untimely death, in 1035 in Shaftsbury, left the issue of his succession unresolved. Cnut had three adult sons: Harthacnut who was his son by Emma of Normandy, and Svein Cnutsson and Harald Harefoot who were his sons by Ælfgifu of Northampton. Cnut had been in a relationship with Ælfgifu before his marriage to Emma, and in this complex situation of political and personal rivalries it was Emma who was the political heavyweight and who out-trumped Ælfgifu. As a result, it was Emma who became queen and Ælfgifu who was forced to play a secondary role. Later, in 1066, Harold Godwinson did the same thing when, after a long relationship with a woman named Edith Swan-neck, he contracted a political marriage with another Edith, the sister of Edwin, Earl of Mercia and Morcar, Earl of Northumbria.

These 'other marriages' were far from casual relationships and, prior to the men in question making more politically advantageous marriages, the women involved were regarded by most people (if not the Church) as being their wives. Contemporaries had a Latin phrase to describe these 'other marriages' and that was marriage *more danico* ('in the Danish manner'). It was regarded as a practice of Scandinavian origin involving a marriage that was not formally recognized by the Church but was in accordance with Scandinavian custom. Such a 'marriage' might be abandoned in favour of marriage to a woman of higher status in a union that was blessed by the Church. There are instances of men returning to their 'wife' *more danico* and, as a consequence, it does not mean that the second marriage completely erased the first one. In addition, children born from a *more danico* relationship could still be regarded as legitimate heirs and taken account of in a father's future planning for the inheritance of land and authority. It was another Viking ingredient that complicated the cocktail of royal politics in England in the eleventh century.

The late eleventh-century historian Adam of Bremen suggests that Cnut had intended Svein Cnutsson to be king of Norway, Harthacnut to be king of Denmark and Harald to be king of England. This certainly would be proof that a *more danico* relationship could produce offspring who were serious contenders when it came to the matter of inheritance. However, the more contemporary source, the *Encomium Emmae Reginae (In Praise of Queen Emma)*, has a different account and claims that when Emma of Normandy agreed to marry Cnut, part of the deal was that it would be her offspring who would take the throne. This does seem to have been the case in Denmark where Cnut sent the eight-year-old Harthacnut to reign in his absence.[1] Given that one of Cnut's key aims in marrying Emma was to neutralize the threat from her sons by Æthelred II, it is highly likely that this agreement would have been part of the marriage contract and not just something made up by the writer of the *Encomium* in order to give the events a spin that suited Emma of Normandy, who was the patron of the compiler of this account.

While this is precisely what one would expect the *Encomium Emmae* to say – Emma was, after all, Harthacnut's mother and if you cannot rely on your mother to push your claim to the throne, who can you rely on? – Harthacnut's primacy over his half-siblings would make sense given the relative power and connections of their mother compared with Ælfgifu of Northampton; Emma was, after all, an ex-queen of England and the sister of the Norman duke. It is also telling that both the C and E manuscripts of the *Anglo-Saxon Chronicle* view Harald Harefoot's claim to the English throne as dubious. Consequently, there is strong evidence to suggest that Harthacnut's stint in Denmark was part of his training for eventually taking over the largest jewel in Cnut's empire, the kingdom of England, as well. Cnut seems to have hoped that his Anglo-Danish Empire was going to continue into the next generation, and that it was to be a Viking future that he bequeathed for his English subjects. So it may be that we should follow the line taken by the writer of the *Encomium* rather than that taken by Adam of Bremen.

However, when Cnut died, in 1035, Harthacnut was in Denmark dealing with the crisis caused by his half-brother, Svein Cnutsson, having been expelled from Norway by Magnus the Good the previous year. Svein had fled to his half-brother in Denmark following his expulsion and he seems to have died shortly afterwards, obviously putting him out of the picture as a contender for the English and Danish thrones. This therefore left the path to the English throne open to Harald Harefoot – Svein Cnutsson's brother – who was the only son in England at the time of Cnut's death. If what we said earlier is correct, this was not what Cnut intended. And it was more than inter-sibling rivalry, for it would have far-flung ramifications that would echo down to 1066 and beyond.

Shortly after Cnut's death, there was a meeting of the leading nobles in Oxford to decide upon the next king. The matter was to prove highly divisive: Earl Leofric of Mercia and many of the northern thegns took up Harald Harefoot's cause, while Godwin of Wessex favoured the absent Harthacnut. In this, Godwin was probably seeking to implement the wishes of the recently deceased Cnut, but Godwin was a shrewd political operator and it is highly probable that he was motivated by more than just loyalty to a dead king's wishes: he was likely motivated by his concern that he would lose the influence and prime position he had so carefully carved out for himself under Cnut.

This division reminds us about the regionalism that was a characteristic of eleventh-century England: the rivalry between Wessex and Mercia and between the two great families who ruled these earldoms. A combination of Harald Harefoot's half-Mercian blood – his mother, Ælfgifu of Northampton, was Mercian – as well as the chance to get one over on Godwin of Wessex led to Leofric supporting Harald Harefoot. As well as this, it has been suggested that in the late 1020s the son of Earl Leofric of Mercia married the daughter of the cousin of Ælfgifu of Northampton.[2] Ælfgifu of Northampton, of course, was Cnut's first wife (*more danico*) and mother of Svein Cnutsson and Harald Harefoot. If correct, this meant that both Earl Leofric and Earl Godwin were related by marriage to Cnut and gave Earl Leofric another reason for throwing the weight of his support behind Harald Harefoot, who was now a kinsman.

Godwin, on the other hand, was keen to support Harthacnut. Through this, we may surmise, he hoped to preserve the *status quo* since he probably felt that an absentee king in Denmark would allow the Earl of Wessex to rule England as regent, a position of authority that he had earlier enjoyed under Cnut. This was a situation that was firmly rooted in the Viking Conquest of 1016, which had entwined England and Denmark so closely together as component parts of Cnut's northern empire. It was also this that had allowed Godwin to rise so fast as

Cnut's loyal henchman. Viking-originating ripples ran far and wide after 1016.

In addition, there also seems to have been some question concerning the paternity of Harald Harefoot: the C, D and E manuscripts of the *Chronicle* all cast aspersions on the legitimacy of his claim to the throne.[3] This was more than just a matter of his parents' marriage *more danico* and seems to have been based on some question over whether Cnut really was his father. It is now difficult to decide whether this doubt was based on evidence or was merely a case of mudslinging in the hope that some would stick to a political rival.

Despite the concerns over Harald Harefoot's paternity, at the Council of Oxford in 1018 it was Godwin's side that lost out. A compromise was reached, which resulted in Harald Harefoot being recognized as king north of the Thames and Harthacnut as king in Wessex. Emma of Normandy was to remain in Winchester and act as regent for Harthacnut. However, the position was difficult to maintain and, despite the compromise, Emma was unable to prevent Harald Harefoot from seizing the royal treasury in Winchester. In the continued absence of Harthacnut, Harald was soon effectively ruling the entire kingdom. Clearly, Harthacnut's problems in Scandinavia were causing him and his mother serious problems in England too. There was only so long that he could remain away and yet still effectively maintain his claim to the throne of England: Denmark was really keeping his eye off the ball, and Harald Harefoot made the most of his half-brother's Scandinavian preoccupations.

There is little in the written record about how this division of the kingdom between Harald and Harthacnut worked out on the ground. However, the numismatic evidence can give us more of an idea regarding its practicalities. There were silver pennies issued by both kings in circulation until 1037. These were comparable coins differentiated by the two separate names. A type known to modern numismatists as the 'Jewel Cross type' was struck with a variable obverse (head-side), on which a left-facing bust (dies cut at London) existed with some bearing the name 'Cnut' and 'Harthacnut' while others carried the name 'Harald'. At the same time a right-facing bust (dies cut at Winchester) carried the name 'Harthacnut'.[4] This sharing of reverse dies suggests a significant degree of cooperation between the two, apparently rival, regimes.

These coins were originally largely minted in the areas where the two kings were supposed to be in control, although it looks as if their spheres of influence overlapped in London. But, as 1036 and 1037 progressed, Harald Harefoot's coins began to be struck south of the Thames – there was no equivalent movement on the part of coin distribution for Harthacnut. Political influence was shifting in favour of the man in residence at the expense of the absentee landlord. The numismatic evidence therefore suggests that, in 1036, Harald became recognized in Wessex, but that Harthacnut's absence was costing him dear and he was failing to make a comparable impact on the north. Earlier cooperation between the two evenly matched administrations was being replaced by a shift in the balance of power in favour of Harald Harefoot.

This shift was not only problematic for Harthacnut; it would also have posed a serious problem for those in England who had backed him. Godwin must have been having serious second thoughts about the wisdom of the position that he had adopted at the Council of Oxford. Without some swift manoeuvring he could find his position in England seriously compromised, as Harald Harefoot and his supporters (most notably Earl Leofric of Mercia) increased the size of their powerbase. After all, the new coins of Harald Harefoot were now being struck in Wessex and that was Godwin's patrimony. Chickens were coming home to roost and Godwin's position, clearly declared at Oxford, was becoming increasingly untenable. The political tension must have been unbearable.

The death of Svein Cnutsson in Denmark in 1036 probably made the situation in Scandinavia even more complex for Harthacnut, who had lost an ally in his conflict with Magnus the Good of Norway. And so, due to the continuing threat of a Norwegian invasion, he was unable to leave Denmark despite the messages from Emma informing him of the urgent need for him to return to England. Harthacnut's failure to come to the aid of his mother put her in an increasingly precarious position with even Godwin starting to look towards Harald Harefoot rather than the absent Harthacnut. Godwin was clearly preparing to jump ship before he lost everything.

The return of the House of Cerdic

In 1036 another challenge to Harald Harefoot's kingship was to emerge, in the form of Emma's sons from her previous marriage to Æthelred II. It is not clear what prompted the æthelings Edward and Alfred to return to England: the *Encomium Emmae* claims that Harald Harefoot's supporters faked a letter to them which purported to originate from their mother calling for them to return to England. Whatever the truth of this, they did return and attempted to meet up with their mother in Winchester. Edward, the elder of the two brothers, came with a fleet of ships but, after a hostile reception in England, quickly returned to Normandy. This proved to be a prudent move.

Alfred came separately to England via Flanders with a band of retainers, which the twelfth-century historian John of Worcester tells us numbered six hundred. According to the *Encomium Emmae*, Alfred refused extra troops offered to him by Count Baldwin of Flanders. What happened next was to have far-reaching repercussions for Godwin's later relationship with Edward when the latter eventually became king. Unfortunately for Alfred, Godwin – who had previously been a supporter of Emma – at that point switched sides. Godwin had risen to power under the Anglo-Danish regime and would consequently have been much more comfortable with the idea of Harald Harefoot as king than Edward or Alfred. If he worried about the strength of his influence under Harald Harefoot he must have been even more alarmed at the prospect of the return of the Anglo-Saxon æthelings, with whom he had no influence whatsoever. For Godwin, it was time to do something decisive but the outcome of the decision that he was about to make was truly shocking.

Godwin and his retainers went to meet Alfred at Guildford, in what initially seemed to have been a friendly manner – after all, Godwin had been a loyal supporter of Alfred's mother, Emma, so it was perhaps not surprising that Alfred trusted him. However, for Alfred, the story does not have a happy ending. Godwin stopped Alfred's progress to Winchester, captured him and blinded him, and had his retainers killed or sold into slavery. Alfred was then cared for by the monks of Ely but shortly afterwards died of his injuries. The different versions of the *Chronicle* have slightly varying accounts of the mutilation of Alfred. While manuscript *C* lays the blame squarely at Godwin's door, manuscript *D* substitutes 'Godwin' with 'he', making it more ambiguous as to whether the guilty party was actually Godwin or Harald Harefoot; it looks like the compiler of manuscript *D* was spinning the retelling in order to partially protect Godwin. On the other hand it is no surprise that the compiler of manuscript *C* was uncompromising in condemning Godwin, since the compiler of this version of the *Chronicle* was probably associated with Leofric of Mercia and adopts an anti-Godwin stance in a number of annals.

What is clear, though, is the universal condemnation of the act itself and the *Chronicle* tells us that 'no more horrible a deed was done in the land since the Danes came and peace was made'.[5] In short, it was the worst thing that had occurred since 1016. This act was to have long-term consequences for Godwin and, whatever the truth behind who ordered the mutilation of Alfred, it is clear that ætheling – and later king – Edward held Godwin personally responsible for his brother's death. This greatly embittered the relationship of Edward with Godwin and had severe implications for England as a whole in the run-up to 1066.

The following year, 1037, Harald Harefoot was declared king over the entirety of England; he is also remembered today as King Harald I. At this point he signalled the final break with his half-brother by minting a new type of coinage, the 'Fleur-de-lis' type. This continued until his early death in 1040.[6]

Harthacnut had been away for too long and loyalties had been strained to breaking point. Consequently, Godwin decided to throw in his lot with Harald Harefoot, and his power and influence enabled Harald to gain recognition across the whole of England. Having achieved unrivalled royal power, Harald I was an unremarkable king. He left no charters, nor any other evidence that he actually did very much during his brief reign. The years 1037–9 do, however, show no serious challenges to his authority so, while unremarkable, Harald I does not seem to have been completely ineffective as a monarch.

The disastrous return of Edward and Alfred made life in England impossible for their mother, Emma: despite remaining in Winchester for a couple of months on Harald I's accession to the entirety of the kingdom of England in 1037, she was eventually forced into exile. The *Chronicle* describes how she was 'driven out without any mercy to face the raging winter'.[7] She went to Bruges where she was welcomed by Count Baldwin, who protected her until the death of Harald I. It is unclear why she fled to Bruges rather than her native Normandy or to her son in Denmark, but it may have been due to the important position Bruges held as a central point in the trade route between Denmark and England.[8] In addition, the suggestion that the count had earlier offered troops to support the return to England of ætheling Alfred indicates that there was a warm relationship between Emma and her exiled sons and the ruler of Flanders.

Adventures in Scandinavia: the Norwegian connection

As previously mentioned, Harthacnut had been in Denmark since 1026 and in the later part of Cnut's reign he seems to have taken over the effective rule of that kingdom. The *Encomium Emmae* and later Norse traditions portray him as King of Denmark even before his father's death, and the numismatic evidence certainly shows him minting coins to that effect.[9] These coins bear a striking resemblance to coins struck by Cnut in England and reveal the close relationship between the royal administrations in England and Denmark that grew up under Cnut and continued into the reign of Harthacnut.[10]

Following the ejection of his half-brother, Svein Cnutsson, from Norway, the kingdom of Norway was ruled by Magnus Olafsson – or Magnus the Good, as he later became known. Magnus was the son of Olaf Haraldsson, a king of Norway who had earlier been deposed with the help of Cnut. As a result his son, Magnus, had an axe to grind (literally as well as figuratively) with whoever Cnut appointed as his proxy in Norway; this was why Svein Cnutsson found himself in difficulties.

Therefore, when Cnut died in 1035 Harthacnut's main concern was not England but the reconquest of Norway, and his invasion preparations were well underway when Svein Cnutsson died unexpectedly in 1036. However, Harthacnut's preparations were slow: he was forced to delay his actions due to the strength of Magnus. By 1040 the strained relations between them had deteriorated to the point that conflict flared up again. Magnus and his advisors gathered their own troops and marched on the northern bank of the Göta river, on the border with Danish territory. This river – also known as the Klar-Göta river – rises in Norway and flows 447 miles (719km) before it reaches Lake Väner (or Vänern) and then flows out of the lake's southern end towards the North Sea. The significance of its location is that it is in south-western Sweden and reminds us that a large part of southern Sweden was ruled by the King of Denmark; it was in what we might refer to as 'Greater Denmark'. It was towards this northern extension of Danish territory that Magnus – based in Norway – directed his attention. However, despite his haste, he was not quite quick enough, and when he arrived Harthacnut was already waiting for him, leaving the stage set for battle. It was 1040 and just five years since the death of Cnut had unsettled the fractious power-politics of Scandinavia.

The most detailed account of what happened next can be found in *Heimskringla* (*Circle of the World*), written in the thirteenth century by Snorri Sturlusson, an Icelandic chieftain. *Heimskringla* is a collection of 'sagas': individual stories chronicling the lives and deeds of the kings of Norway. Snorri tells us that due to the relative youth of the two kings they were greatly influenced by their advisors. Many of these advisors had friends and relatives in the opposing armies, and they arranged for the kings to meet in order to avoid bloodshed if at all possible. During this meeting a peace treaty was proposed. This treaty suggested a 'brotherly union under oath' between the two kings, meaning that they would live in peace for the rest of their lives and that if one should die without a son then the other would be his successor.[11] It seems likely that, prior to these negotiations, Harthacnut had already recognized the difficulty he faced in forcing the Norwegians back into subjection to the Danes. This had been difficult enough to achieve under his father, and Harthacnut did not have the political might of Cnut. As a result of this meeting, a peace was achieved that secured Norway for Magnus while freeing Greater Denmark from the threat of Norwegian invasion. Harthacnut now had a friendly neighbour in Norway and could turn his attention away from that distraction and towards increasing the security and prosperity of Denmark.

Although highly important to Danish and Norwegian interests in 1040, the Göta River Agreement may seem to be merely a footnote in the history of Scandinavia in the eleventh century, a forgotten piece of Viking *Realpolitik*. However, although it ensured peace while the two kings were still alive, this 'footnote' was to have unforeseen consequences in England, of all places, twenty-six years later. Harthacnut died childless and, as a result, Denmark was claimed by King Magnus. This was a logical outcome of the Göta River Agreement. However, this southern extension of Magnus' authority was opposed by Svein Estrithson – Harthacnut's cousin – who fought Magnus' rule in Denmark until 1045, when Magnus' uncle Harald Hardrada returned to Norway from exile. Svein Estrithson had originally been appointed Magnus' regent in Denmark after Harthacnut's death in 1042, but had soon become too independent and Magnus had driven him out. Svein Estrithson, unsurprisingly, had not accepted this and conflict continued until the unexpected return of Harald Hardrada. His arrival was a game-changer.

Harald Hardrada was a brutal ruler and an experienced warrior. He had fought from Scandinavia to the Mediterranean. There, for a time (while in exile) he had served in the Varangian Guard of the Byzantine emperor. Harald Hardrada and Svein Estrithson joined forces and forced Magnus to share the Norwegian throne with Hardrada. This power-sharing arrangement was short-lived as Magnus died in 1047, having stated on his deathbed that his kingdom should be divided: Harald Hardrada would get the throne of Norway, while Svein Estrithson would be King of Denmark.

It is therefore by this circuitous route that Harald Hardrada claimed to have the right to the English throne. When Harthacnut died in 1042, King Magnus claimed that the terms of the Göta River Agreement should be extended to include all of Harthacnut's possessions and, since Harthacnut was King of England when he died, it should also include the English crown. This was despite the facts that Harthacnut was not actually King of England when the agreement had been made in 1040 and that England was not within Harthacnut's gift to give anyway. However, the throne went not to Magnus but to Edward the Confessor. At this point, Magnus reportedly wrote to King Edward informing him that he would be launching a combined Danish-Norwegian invasion of England – but this invasion never materialized. On Magnus' death in 1047 it seemed that this threat had been neutralized, but memories are long and nineteen years later this agreement, made between participants then long dead, would have consequences neither of them could ever have imagined. In 1066, Harald Hardrada thought that he had a right to the throne of England, inherited from Magnus; it was a convoluted route that led him to this claim, but this route started in the Göta River Agreement of 1040.

The return of Harthacnut

The two years following Harthacnut's peace treaty with Magnus were quieter years in Denmark. This peace was also cemented by the marriage of Harthacnut's sister, Gunnhild, to Henry, son of Holy Roman Emperor Conrad. This meant that both Denmark's borders with Germany and with Norway were, for the first time in many years, secure. Like his father before him Harthacnut thought beyond his country's borders, and Adam of Bremen tells us how he maintained a good relationship with the dukes of Saxony, the Slav princes of Vendland/Wendland (on the southern Baltic Coast) and with Count Baldwin of Flanders – where his mother was in exile. Clearly, he took diplomacy seriously.

There is evidence that Harthancnut visited his mother in exile, with the *Encomium* describing him as being accompanied by a small fleet of ships that was threatened by a storm on the way to Flanders. The *Encomium* describes how Harthacnut was protected by God during the storm and that a divine message was given to him in a dream, which promised success if he were to invade England. The *Encomium* also outlines how, during this visit to Flanders, Emma shared with Harthacnut the details of Harald I (Harefoot)'s involvement in the death of ætheling Alfred, describing how his anger at this drove him to promise to avenge the death of his murdered half-brother.

However, despite his outrage, Harthacnut did not invade and it may well be that he decided that – given the poor health of Harald I – it was worth waiting it out until his death rather than risking an invasion. What does seem clear, though, is that he was in Flanders in 1039 – this is reported by both the *Chronicle* and the *Encomium* – and he is likely to have used this opportunity to open lines of communication with the English nobility. That he did so seems clear from the fact that his eventual succession occurred very smoothly. Harthacnut did not have to wait long and when Harald I died in Oxford on 17 March 1040, the English earls sent for Harthacnut. So it was that, in June 1040, Harthacnut landed in England and finally claimed the throne for himself. It was a position that he had worked for since the death of Cnut in 1035.

It is significant that one of Harthacnut's first acts as king was to seek vengeance on his dead half-brother and to have his body disinterred – Harald I had been buried at Westminster – and thrown into a marsh. Whether this was due to Harald's role in the death of Alfred or to his taking of the whole kingdom of England and sending Emma into exile is unclear, but it certainly shows that there was no brotherly love lost between Harald and Harthacnut. Emma's revenge took the form of commissioning the writing of the *Encomium Emmae Reginae*, which presented the history of this troubled time as seen from her perspective. Clearly, between the literal marsh chosen by Harthacnut and the literary 'marsh' constructed by Emma, Harald I's significance and reputation would struggle to be recognized after his death.

In this politically charged atmosphere, Godwin moved quickly to secure his own position. As the man who had backed and then abandoned Harthacnut and who, furthermore, had been complicit (at least) in the mutilation and death of Harthacnut's half-brother Alfred, Godwin had a lot of lost ground to make up. He did so by swearing on oath that he was innocent with regard to Alfred's death and that the man responsible was Harald I. Godwin then followed this by offering a massive sweetener to the new king in the form of a magnificent warship, fully equipped and manned by eighty picked warriors. We know nothing of these astute moves from contemporary sources, but learn of them from the twelfth-century historian, John of Worcester, in his *Chronicon ex Chronicis* (*Chronicle of other Chronicles*). Since John of Worcester seems well informed, from access to traditions now lost to us, it is highly likely that this is what Godwin did.

Things did not go smoothly for England under the new king. Harthacnut imposed a very heavy tax on the English upon his arrival, in order to pay for his ships and warriors; he had arrived with sixty ships and a retinue of around 5,000 men. This was an incredibly large force in a country where the population of London, the largest city, only numbered around 10,000 people. This was not the act of a new king who saw himself as welcomed in by his subjects; rather, it was a show of strength, the act of a man who saw himself as a conqueror and the people of England as a conquered people.[12] Clearly it rankled with him that many among the English elite had backed Harald Harefoot back in 1035. The *Chronicle* tells us that the tax was paid in 1041 and this amounted to £21,099 and that a further £11,000 was paid to retain a standing navy of thirty-two ships. These were vast sums of money. Resentment concerning this tax was revealed in Worcestershire where, in May 1041, the inhabitants killed two of Harthacnut's *huscarls* (royal household troops) who attempted to impose it on the area. This led to the county being ravaged. Economic problems were compounded by a 'galloping inflation' that characterized the reign of Harthacnut.[13]

Another of the black marks against Harthacnut's name was the killing of Earl Eadwulf of Bernicia in 1041. It is unclear exactly what Eadwulf did to earn Harthacnut's wrath, but the *Chronicle* tells us that he betrayed Eadwulf after guaranteeing his safety and that he, therefore, became an oath breaker. In an age that took the swearing of oaths very seriously (Harold Godwinson was to get into a lot of trouble by breaking one made to William of Normandy) this was a serious sin and breach of trust. The combination of the high taxes and heavy-handed rule did not go down well in England, and the C and D manuscripts of the *Chronicle* tell us that 'he did nothing worthy of a king as long as he ruled'.[14]

However, it would not be entirely fair to dismiss Harthacnut completely since he does seem to have followed in his father's footsteps in being a generous benefactor to the Church. In 1042, he granted land to the Bishop of Winchester and he also issued two writs in favour of the Abbey of Ramsey in Cambridgeshire. One of these is particularly interesting as it was made jointly with his mother and gave the land 'for the soul of our dear lord, King Cnut'. This shows Harthacnut working closely with his mother, which is perhaps not surprising given how politically astute Emma had proved herself to be in the past.[15]

In 1041, faced with the lack of an heir and possibly anticipating an early death – it has been suggested that Harthacnut had been suffering from tuberculosis for a number of years – as well as the need to bolster his unpopular regime, Harthacnut recalled his half-brother, ætheling Edward (son of Æthelred II), from his exile in Normandy.[16] Harthacnut did not reign long after this as, in 1042, he died. The *Chronicle* states that 'he was standing at his drink and he suddenly fell to the ground with fearful convulsions, and those who were near caught him, and he spoke no word afterwards'.[17] He had been king of England for just over two years. He was then taken and buried in the Old Minster, Winchester, next to his father King Cnut.

Thus the Anglo-Danish period came to an end in England, not with a bang but with a whimper. Despite the military prowess and strength of Svein Forkbeard and Cnut, the early deaths of all three of Cnut's sons and the lack of any direct heirs meant that Cnut's dynasty had to come to a sudden halt, and his empire was now to be swiftly dismantled. The death of Harthacnut meant that the ancient Anglo-Saxon royal house of Cerdic, under the man later titled Edward the Confessor, was once again ruling the English nation. However, although Viking rule was over, its repercussions would continue for some time. They would influence key features of the reign of Edward the Confessor and would eventually lead to the end of Anglo-Saxon England in 1066.

The unforeseen consequences of Danish rule

It was the Cnut's creation of the Scandinavian connection that led to the unsuccessful invasion of England by the Norwegian king, Harald Hardrada, in September 1066. Harald Hardrada's belief in his right to the throne could never have occurred if an English king had been on the throne for the entirety of the eleventh century.

In addition, the rapid succession of kings after Cnut's death in 1035 led to a 'long term fragility of the royal kin and the breakdown of its monopoly of kingship'.[18] The succession of a non-royal to the throne before the reign of Cnut would have been unthinkable, but this undermining of the authority of the English royal line between 1035 and 1042 meant that by January 1066, when Edward the Confessor died, Harold Godwinson was able to take the throne instead of the rightful royal candidate, Edgar Ætheling; this led to 'the dramatic events of the remainder of the year'.[19] In the previous century, despite the youth of both Æthelred II and his half-brother, Edward King and Martyr, they had still been anointed as kings: their royal legitimacy was enough to outweigh the disadvantage associated with their age. However, as we shall see in due course, Edgar

Ætheling's minority led to the acceptance, in January 1066, of a non-royal.

This was an unintended but direct consequence of the chain of events set in motion by the Viking conquest of England in 1016 under Cnut. Exactly how this was to occur will be explored in Chapter 8. However, we first need to investigate exactly what happened to the young children of Edmund Ironside during these years of Viking rule in England. For that, too, was to have profound implications for what would eventually transpire in 1066. It is to that investigation that we will now turn.

CHAPTER 7

Home Thoughts from Abroad: A Postcard from Hungary

When Cnut came to power in 1016, his accession led to the children of the last Anglo-Saxon king, Edmund Ironside, being taken out of the country. They eventually ended up in Hungary: only at that kind of distance from England were they judged to be safe from the long arm of Cnut's potentially murderous influence. They would not return to England until the 1050s.

Today the distance by road between London and Budapest (Hungary's capital) is about 1,070 miles by the most direct route. A horse might achieve an average distance of 20 miles a day and perhaps more if rested, with a substitute horse used on a rotating basis. This is very approximate but a reasonable working figure, since most so-called 'long riders' achieve about 20 miles per day when both horse and rider are in good condition.[1] On this basis, the journey to London would take fifty-four days. Even if doing the journey at the speed of the fastest historic riders (the Mongols or the US Pony Express) – who achieved 100 miles a day by swapping horses about every 20 miles – the journey would take eleven days, and this is not a feasible figure as a journey-time in the 1050s.

By way of contrast, the sailing distance between London and Esbjerg on the Danish coast is 402 nautical miles (463 statute miles) by the most direct route. At 10 knots this could be achieved in about 1 day and 16 hours.[2] It is difficult to be precise about eleventh-century sailing speeds, but a maximum speed, under favourable conditions, for a Viking long-ship was probably 15 knots, so 10 knots is a reasonable working speed for this calculation.

The implication is clear: it is a very long way to Hungary. While journeying there, as we shall shortly see, the exiles took an even longer and more circuitous route. When, eventually, the survivors returned we may assume that the route was rather more direct. Either way, their place of exile was a very long way from their homeland in England, and this was to have important repercussions for the history of eleventh-century England.

The evidence for what happened to the children of Edmund Ironside

Æthelred II's children by Emma of Normandy (æthelings Alfred and Edward) fled to Normandy when Cnut came to power. However, Æthelred II's son by a previous marriage was Edmund Ironside and, as he was older than his half-brothers, he succeeded to the crown when Æthelred died in 1016. However, as we saw in Chapter 2 he himself died later that same year, after he had fought Cnut to a bloody stalemate.

Edmund Ironside left behind two infant children, who are remembered as Edward Ætheling and Edmund Ætheling. The Old English title 'ætheling' indicates that the bearer of the title was of royal blood and throne-worthy (i.e. they were eligible to be king). Edmund Ironside's brother, Eadwig Ætheling, was another such royal, from the generation above that of Edward Ætheling and Edmund Ætheling; however, as we have seen in Chapter 3, this uncle of the two younger æthelings was murdered, on Cnut's orders, following his being sent into exile in 1017. This reduces the number of æthelings that we need to bear in mind.

Not surprisingly, given the multiple consecutive marriages that occurred (or even the concurrent ones in the case of Cnut!) there was often a surfeit of æthelings with a claim to the throne. As we have seen in the case of the half-brothers Harald I Harefoot and Harthacnut, this did not always lead to sibling harmony. But to return to the case of the children, Edward Ætheling and Edmund Ætheling in the aftermath of the Viking Conquest of 1016, we are reminded of how Cnut combined a shrewd political judgement and Christian religious orthodoxy with a ruthless pursuit of *Realpolitik*. The same person who made a gift of a gold cross to the church at Winchester could also carry out a bloody purge of those who threatened his power. And Cnut, as a ruler who had taken power through the sword, faced real future trouble in the shape of the two little æthelings: each had an impeccable claim to the English throne, and the royal blood of Alfred the Great flowed through their veins. It, though, might be more useful, from Cnut's perspective, if it flowed onto the floor! The æthelings' fate in the period 1016–54 would entangle the royal families of England, Denmark, Sweden, Russia and Hungary. It is a story of distant places of exile and of eventual return. And in this story, their fate was a direct consequence of the Viking Conquest of 1016 and would be one of the ingredients that led to the Norman Conquest of 1066. It was yet another of those causal factors that linked 1016, and its aftermath, with the later events that shook England in 1066.

The *Anglo-Saxon Chronicle*'s annals for the period including the end of the reign of Æthelred II's and Cnut's conquest were probably written in London during the early years of the reign of Cnut.[3] It has nothing to say about the fate of Edward Ætheling and Edmund Ætheling. The *Chronicle* entry for 1017 simply records: 'King Cnut exiled the ætheling

Eadwig and afterwards had him killed.[4] To this the later chronicler, John of Worcester, added a key piece of information so that it flowed directly from this statement of Cnut's ruthlessness in killing Eadwig Ætheling:

> Eadric [Streona] advised him [Cnut] to kill also the young æthelings, Edward and Edmund, the sons of King Edmund [Ironside]; but because it would be a great disgrace to him for them to perish in England, he sent them after a short passage of time to the king of the Swedes to be killed. He would by no means acquiesce in his requests, although there was a treaty between them, but sent them to the king of the Hungarians, Solomon by name, to be preserved and brought up there.[5]

John of Worcester then goes on to say that in Hungary, Edmund Ætheling died but that Edward Ætheling married a woman named Agatha, the daughter of the brother of the Holy Roman Emperor Henry III (reigned 1017–56). If true, this allied him to a powerful European royal family since the Holy Roman Empire (as it has since come to be generally known, though technically it was only so called from 1254), at this point in time dominated central Europe from the Baltic to northern Italy. From this marriage they had three children: Margaret (who later married the king of Scots), Christina (who became a nun) and Edgar Ætheling.

The tradition that Cnut resisted Eadric Streona's suggestion that the boys be immediately killed is also found in the record made by Simeon of Durham. He wrote his *Historia Regum* (*History of the Kings*) in the mid to late twelfth century and recorded an identical account of the fate of the two young princes. However, the close similarity between his work and that of John of Worcester means that it cannot be read as corroborative evidence, since it is clear that he derived his information from John of Worcester's *Chronicon ex Chronicis* (*Chronicle of other Chronicles*), completed shortly after 1140.

It is conventional to call Edward Ætheling 'Edward the Exile' after his exile to Hungary and so it is now 'Edward the Exile' and his foreign-born son, Edgar Ætheling that we will follow in their exile and then eventual return to England, when they were to play their part in the unsettled politics that led to 1066.

First, though, it is worth asking: from where did John of Worcester get his information that enabled him to detail the extent of the 1017 purge, that was truncated in the *Chronicle* account? The answer is that part, at least, came from manuscript *D* of the *Chronicle*; this was compiled later than the more discreet annal of the *Chronicle*, which was written concerning the events of 1017 (manuscript C). Manuscript *D* refers to events in 1057 when Edward the Exile and Edgar Ætheling finally returned to England. The annal for that year states that Edward the Exile (and, we must surmise from his later appearances, Edgar Ætheling) returned to England from Hungary, to where they had been banished by Cnut. It goes on to say that, while in Hungary, Edward the Exile married the emperor's niece.[6]

This is jumping ahead in our story (*see* Chapter 8), but it is worth pausing here because problems in the sources mean that we struggle to get a clear picture of the circumstances leading to the Hungarian exile of these Anglo-Saxon royals. This is evident in the fact that in its account of 1057, manuscript *D* of the *Chronicle* makes no mention of the journey to Sweden or the humane actions of the king of the Swedes that feature so prominently in the account of John of Worcester regarding the events of 1017. So, from where did John of Worcester derive his story of the Swedish interlude?

John of Worcester based his work on the *Chronicon* (usually referred to as the *Universal History*) compiled on the continent by Marianus Scotus, of Mainz, which recounted history from the creation to 1082). This work, though, contains very little information on England and so John expanded the account by drawing on other sources. These included: the writings of the early eighth-century Anglo-Saxon monk Bede and of Alfred the Great's biographer, the Welsh Bishop Asser; various accounts of the lives of English saints; Anglo-Saxon laws; the *Anglo-Saxon Chronicle*; and also records and traditions found in the archive of the major Christian centre at Worcester in the late eleventh and early twelfth centuries. It is presumably from this last source that the tradition of the Swedish leg of the journey into exile was drawn.

Aspects of John of Worcester's account sound legendary: the young princes are sent into exile and unbeknown to them they are accompanied by a message of death; the hapless foreign subservient ruler who is tasked with carrying out the bloody deed; the revolt of conscience by that ruler; the secret sending of the innocent youths to a place of safety in a distant land. Nevertheless, something did happen and it cannot all be dismissed as literary fiction. The two youths *were* clearly sent from England and, somehow, ended up in Hungary. And Hungary is a very long way off. In this case it is actually possible that the stuff of legend was the stuff of history. It is clear that Cnut had a long reach and much influence; he was not a ruler to be trifled with, and somewhere like Hungary might have been necessary to make the young æthelings 'vanish'. The *Chronicle* entry for 1057 suggests that they were sent to Hungary in order to be betrayed; John of Worcester believed that betrayal was to have occurred in Sweden and that Hungary became a place of refuge. Either way, the rather garbled accounts still agree that betrayal was the intention and that somehow the children survived the plan to murder them.

Although the *Chronicle* is sparse in its treatment of the material, we can pick up something of what happened from other, later, written sources. These do, though, have to be treated with caution as the origins of some of the traditions recorded in them are far from clear, and some have clearly undergone considerable embellishment in order to fill out the bare bones of the story of the dramatic exile to Hungary. One of these sources was written by Geoffrey Gaimar, who was active in the mid-1130s (and so a contemporary of John of Worcester). In his *L'Estoire des Engleis* (*History of the English*) – written c.1136–40, in rhymed French couplets – he drew on the *Anglo-Saxon Chronicle* and other late eleventh- and early twelfth-century traditions.

Gaimar adds the intriguing comment that in exiling the two young æthelings, Cnut was acting on the advice of his wife Emma (previously the wife of Æthelred II and so the step-grandmother of the young boys). He also claimed that, before going on to Sweden, they were first taken to Denmark by a Danish nobleman named Walgar and remained there for twelve years. This is less convincing than it sounds because, as one expert who studied Gaimar extensively has concluded regarding his account of events between 959 and 1100, it is 'history seen through the eyes of romance' and furthermore Gaimar is often 'led astray by his love of legends and eulogy'.[7] This is almost certainly true of Gaimar's unique record that blames Emma for the actions of Cnut. In fact, Cnut was more than capable of ruthless bloodletting without it being suggested to him by his new wife. It also sounds rather too likely to have been constructed by Gaimar or his sources to shift the blame for this planned infanticide away from Cnut and onto the stock hate-figure of the 'scheming woman'. And this is all too likely in the context of twelfth-century gender politics.

On the other hand, the suggestion that the move to Sweden went via Denmark is not unique to Gaimar. It is also found in the record compiled by the Anglo-Norman chronicler Orderic Vitalis (1075–c.1142) in his *Historia Ecclesiastica* (the *History of the Church*), which he compiled in Normandy between 1114 and 1141. It is a record of the Normans and their conquests, and includes detailed accounts of the lives of people at a range of social levels. Orderic drew on information from a number of contemporary Norman historians and his work is a more convincing source than the populist work produced by Gaimar. Nevertheless, Orderic had a keen sense of detail and dramatic incidents and, unusually for such a compilation, his work unites learned comment with popular stories. This may well explain the attention to detail regarding the journey into exile. The information that Orderic and Gaimar have in common about the stop-over in Denmark is probably drawn from a common tradition that both of them accessed, since both were writing at about the same time. The existence of such traditions explains the fact that an account of the planned murder-by-proxy is also found in William of Malmesbury's *Gesta regum Anglorum* (*Deeds of the Kings of the English*), written in about 1125. However, in this account, William mistakenly calls Edmund Ætheling 'Edwy'.

Like Gaimar, Orderic Vitalis also recorded snippets of information that are unique to his account. Sadly, these do not inspire confidence in his source since he got the names of the æthelings wrong, incorrectly named the ruler of Denmark at this time as Sweyn, says that the æthelings were sent to the king of the Huns, and finally that Edward became King of Hungary. The penultimate point may have been an understandable conflation of Huns/Hungary, but the final point is simply wrong.

The æthelings in Hungary ... or was that Kiev?

Gaimar says that the æthelings travelled from Sweden to Russia, through which they travelled for five days, until they reached a settlement that Gaimar called 'Gardimbre'. There they were met by the Hungarian king, who was accompanied by his wife. Having settled in Hungary, Gaimar records that the elder ætheling married the king's daughter and was made heir to the throne of Hungary (there are echoes of Orderic Vitalis' account here). In an unbelievable episode Gaimar brings Edward the Confessor to Hungary in the period that he himself was in exile in Normandy, in order to assist his relatives against their enemies (the people of 'Velacase').

There have been suggestions that the young æthelings were taken from Sweden to Kiev before eventually ending up in Hungary.[8] This argument rests on a number of points: there was a well-established Viking connection between the Baltic and the Black Sea via Russia and Kiev; the King of Sweden was related by marriage to the ruler of Kiev; in 1029, King Olaf of Norway was forced to flee to Russia to escape Cnut; the German chronicler Adam of Bremen, writing between 1073 and 1076, claims that the æthelings were taken to Russia; and Gaimar's settlement called 'Gardimbre' is probably best interpreted as representing a confused form of 'Gardar rike', a settlement on Lake Ladoga in Russia that was founded by the ninth-century Viking adventurer Rurik. There is also a reference to exile in Russia found in the so-called *Leges Edwardi Confessoris* (*Laws of Edward the Confessor*).[9] This is an early twelfth-century commentary on English law that claims – erroneously – to be based on a document dating from just after the Norman Conquest in 1066.

If this is correct, their journey into exile was via Denmark, Sweden, Russia and eventually to Hungary. Beyond this it is difficult to be more precise in investigating their time abroad, despite the presence of much later legends that purport to refer to their stay there. Clearly, though, while in Kiev or in Hungary, Edward the Exile married Agatha. She is variously described as: a relative of the Holy Roman Emperor (in the *Chronicle*, John of Worcester and Simeon of Durham; although Ailred of Rievaulx, in the 1150s, was more specific and said she was his daughter and Matthew Paris, in the first half of the thirteenth century, said she was his sister); a daughter of the King of Hungary (Orderic Vitalis,

Gaimar); a sister of the Hungarian queen (William of Malmesbury); and a women of noble or royal family in Kievan Russia (the *Leges Edwardi Confessoris* and Roger of Howden, who died in 1201). The range of options is rather striking, to put it mildly. What is beyond dispute is that Edward the Exile became drawn by marriage into the power politics of central Europe. And there he might have remained, had events not taken a surprising turn.

Home thoughts from abroad ... the return of Edward the Exile and Edgar Ætheling

As we shall shortly see (in Chapter 8), the mid-1050s was a critical time in English politics. Edward the Confessor had no heir. Who would eventually succeed him? There were various candidates and the politics of it all were getting complex. Norman friends of Edward the Confessor were supporting the candidature of Duke William of Normandy. Svein Estrithson, King of Denmark, had a claim via his family connection with Cnut. In Norway, Harald Hardrada nursed a claim based on the agreement made between his predecessor, Magnus the Good, and Harthacnut. Ralph of Mantes was Edward the Confessor's nephew by his sister Godgifu and, as a significant noble, he held land on the borders with Wales.

Into this mix was thrown the person of Edward the Exile. He was a full-blooded Anglo-Saxon royal and as such trumped all the others. In addition, he had already fathered an heir – Edgar Ætheling – and so could promise a smooth succession into the next generation. Those among his contemporaries who considered him a viable candidate could take encouragement from other European exiles who had succeeded in returning from exile and had successfully re-established themselves: Andrew of Hungary, Magnus the Good of Norway and Edward the Confessor himself. There were precedents. It was in this context that moves were set in train to bring Edward the Exile and his family home from Hungary.

In 1054, Ealdred, Bishop of Worcester, was dispatched 'to Cologne on the king's business'[10] and was received there by the Emperor Henry III. He remained there for nearly a year. If we only had the *Chronicle* we would not know the purpose of this visit, but John of Worcester informs us that the purpose was to secure the return of Edward the Exile. Interestingly, William of Malmesbury states that the mission was sent directly to Hungary and makes no mention of the bishop's travels to Cologne. He does, though, specifically claim that Edward the Exile was at this time considered to be the heir to the English throne and that this was acknowledged by Edward the Confessor. This status is likewise found in Gaimar's account and also in the so-called *Dunfermline Vita* [Life] of St *Margaret of Scotland*, written in the thirteenth century, which also says that the initial move was via the emperor in Germany. (St Margaret was the daughter of Edward the Exile.)

It is a reasonable assumption that the preferred strategy did involve meeting with the emperor. Henry III was related to Edward the Confessor, having married Edward's half-sister Gunhild (his first wife, who died in 1038), who had been the child of Cnut and Emma. This marriage alliance had been of mutual benefit as it was designed to limit the growing power of Flanders. In addition, the claim in the *Chronicle* that Agatha (Edward the Exile's wife) was a relative of Emperor Henry III would have further made it a shrewd move to involve the emperor in any plans involving his relative. There is evidence that Henry took a very real interest in such family marriages and arrangements, since they involved alliances that might affect his power.

Furthermore, in 1054 Henry III was particularly sensitive with regard to Hungary. King Andrew I of Hungary had recently (in 1046) deposed and blinded Henry III's vassal, King Peter Orseolo, and this had led to conflict between the emperor and the Hungarians in 1051 and 1052. To add to this, Conrad of Bavaria had rebelled against Henry III and then sought shelter in Hungary. In this context it is clear that things Hungarian were high on Henry III's agenda in 1054, and not in a positive way. On the other hand, it is likely that Andrew I of Hungary was not in a frame of mind to facilitate diplomatic missions from England that came with the blessing of the emperor. Edward the Exile and his family had suddenly become 'another possible pawn in ongoing negotiations' and, as 'diplomatic bargaining chips',[11] the negotiations regarding them would have been far from straightforward, and may explain both the length of Bishop Ealdred's mission abroad and its eventual failure.

By 1057, though, the political tectonic plates had shifted: Henry III had died in 1056; peaceful relations had been established between the imperial government and Baldwin of Flanders following Henry III's death; and the imperial relationship with Hungary was slowly thawing. Andrew I of Hungary was facing competition from his brother over the succession and, in response, crowned his own young son, Salomon, in order to block his brother's ambitions. Improving relationships with the empire was a shrewd move at this time of internal tensions within Hungary, so a peace treaty was established in 1058; in 1059, Salomon was betrothed to Judith, the daughter of Agnes, the imperial regent and the sister of the next emperor, Henry IV. Andrew I's act of 'releasing the English heir as a gesture of goodwill'[12] was almost certainly a product of this changing relationship with the empire. So, it was the power-politics of central Europe that finally made it possible for Edward the Exile and his son Edgar Ætheling to return to England.

In a further twist in the tale, it is likely that Harold Godwinson, Earl of Wessex (who was a leading figure in the events of 1066), played a part in this return. In 1056, he led a diplomatic mission to the continent on behalf of Edward the Confessor. We know he was in Saint-Omer (Flanders) in November 1056 and from there he probably travelled to Regensburg, via Ghent, St Ghislain, Aachen, Cologne and Worms. A particularly fascinating piece of detective work lies behind this hypothetical itinerary, based on the sacred relics housed at Harold Godwinson's much patronised abbey at Waltham (Essex);[13] these suggest that a relic-gathering tour occurred in the 1050s that involved the places mentioned above. In addition, there is no evidence that Harold Godwinson was in England between November 1056 and the return of Edward the Exile and Edgar Ætheling in 1057.

The evidence overall is circumstantial but still persuasive. It seems that Harold Godwinson was tasked by Edward the Confessor with arranging the homecoming of the exiles. If correct, this entwines two of the key players in the drama of 1066: Harold Godwinson and Edgar Ætheling. And this was a weaving together of political actors that was a direct result of Cnut's Viking Conquest of 1016. Without that event, Edward the Exile and his son would not have been in exile and Harold Godwinson would have merely been the successor to a middle-ranking Sussex landowner. It was 1016 that changed all that. And the repercussions went further, for the impeccable throne-worthiness of the exiles had been undermined by the period of exile.

That Edward the Exile's candidature was seriously weakened by his period of exile is undeniable. It is doubtful whether he spoke English fluently. Furthermore, he was married to a foreign princess and so was not integrated into the English political system. Marriage to Agatha may have counted in the politics of Hungary but would have cut little ice in the complicated political manoeuvrings necessary to reintegrate into England. The absence of a marital alliance with another of the leading elite families in England cost Edward the Exile allies that he could not afford to be without. All in all, it meant that when the exiles returned in 1057 they were coming back to an alien political landscape, within which their room for manoeuvre was severely curtailed. It did not bode well for the future political influence of Edward and Edgar, and this was yet another unforeseen consequence of Cnut's seizure of power in 1016. As a result, in the decade leading up to 1066, non-royals like the Godwinsons wielded substantially more political influence than pure-blooded Anglo-Saxon royals such as Edward the Exile and his son. This would have far-reaching ramifications in January 1066, when Edward the Confessor died.

CHAPTER 8

Happy Families, Unhappy King: The Reign of Edward the Confessor

The reign of King Edward (today remembered as 'Edward the Confessor') lasted from 1042 until his death in January 1066. He inherited a kingdom that had been under the rule of a Danish dynasty since 1016. As we have seen, first Cnut (ruled 1016–35), then Harald I Harefoot (ruled 1035–40) and finally Harthacnut (ruled Denmark 1035–42 and then England and Denmark 1040–42) had sat on the throne of England. This Danish or Anglo-Danish rule had been made possible by Cnut's 'Viking Conquest' of 1016 and had a profound effect on the politics of England in the period of Edward the Confessor's reign. It was not, of course, the only ingredient within that cocktail of turbulence, but it was undoubtedly the single most potent one. And its effects ran in a wide range of directions and at a number of levels.

The inheritance of Edward the Confessor

Anglo-Danish rule had effectively marginalized throne-worthy Anglo-Saxons from English politics (Edward the Exile, ætheling Edward – the Confessor – and his brother, ætheling Alfred) for over two decades. Only toward the end of this 26-year period had Harthacnut brought ætheling Edward back into the political limelight and then it was as one who had to reintegrate himself into the court politics of England. And it was to be a further fourteen years before Edward the Exile would set foot again on English soil, and he would then arrive as a total stranger despite his impeccable royal credentials.

Furthermore, the period of the Viking Wars under Æthelred II and Edmund Ironside, and the subsequent years of Danish rule, had fractured old political loyalties in England, removed old players in the political game and had raised new men whose power was a curious combination of insecurity and ferocious ambition (most notably Godwin and the Godwinsons) and yet, in a period of shifting allegiances and a semi-change of dynasty in 1042, they stood in powerful positions that could challenge – or at least unsettle – a ruler who was not as integrated into the power-politics of England as they were. The rule of Cnut meant that the returning ætheling Edward could not ignore or fully control the powerful Godwin family (*see* Chapter 4). An unintended consequence of the Viking Conquest of 1016 and the creation of Cnut's Anglo-Danish Empire had been the creation of these at first insecure, but in time over-mighty, subjects, and this chapter will explore how Edward's eventual resentment towards them flared into open conflict, and how this in turn deepened and complicated the Norman connection.

Then there was that 'Norman connection'. This can be overstated but, as we shall see, the rule of King Edward the Confessor (once an exile in Normandy) saw both the advancement of Normans and other French-men within aspects of Anglo-Saxon church and government, alongside the growing candidature of the Norman duke himself for the position of Edward's heir and inheritor of the crown of England. Not all of this was an invention of pro-Norman chroniclers in the decades after 1066; this was a plant that certainly had roots reaching down into the events of the 1050s; and these were themselves derived from a 'taproot' that extended back into ætheling Edward's youth. Without the Viking-enforced exile in Normandy (*see* Chapter 5) such a situation would not have developed.

As we explore the events of Edward the Confessor's reign we will see, amid the shadows and obfuscation, the increasing significance of these factors and their causal connections with what came next in the proc-esses leading to the traumatic events of the year 1066.

The return of the king

Edward was forty-seven years old when he came to the throne and had spent most of his life in exile at the Norman court. This was due to his connection with that dukedom through his Norman mother, Emma, the wife not only of Æthelred II but also of Cnut. As a consequence, Edward had far more foreign connections, allegiances and influences than any previous king of Anglo-Saxon England. It also meant that he was politi-cally very inexperienced, having been isolated from English politics for twenty-five years. The situation he found himself in as king was very different to the English political system his father had managed, however well we may judge his success in this task. Given the speed with which Anglo-Saxon England unravelled on the death of King Edward in Janu-ary 1066, we cannot separate the events of his reign from the events of the year following his death. Nor can we separate his reign from the period between 1016 and 1042, which established the political landscape on which his rule would be enacted.

As we saw in Chapter 6, towards the end of his reign (and life) Harthac-nut invited ætheling Edward – his half-brother – back to England from exile in Normandy. As a consequence, when Harthacnut died suddenly in 1042, Edward was suddenly propelled from royal-hopeful to King of England. After the years in exile in Normandy the turnaround in his political status was truly remarkable.

Despite late Anglo-Saxon England having the most senior royal line in Europe it had – surprisingly – no clear-cut procedure for choosing a new king.[1] Obviously, eligibility by birth was extremely important (which also, in the eleventh century, meant a male candidate). However, it was not the only factor and in a period of history marked by successive (and in Cnut's case concurrent) marriages there might be multiple male descendants with a claim and, in the memorable words of Kenneth Harrison, on the death of a king 'the hungry æthelings began to prowl'.[2]

Designation by the previous king was also an important route to power and, as we shall see, this was to be a crucial and controversial factor in the events leading to 1066. But this could not be translated into real or secure royal authority without the recognition (often termed 'election') provided by the senior elite landowners and Church leaders. And then this was transformed into (theoretically) unassailable royal authority when followed by being crowned, anointed and consecrated by the senior representative(s) of the Church in England – most obviously the Archbishop of Canterbury, although the Archbishop of York might suffice if Canterbury was indisposed or ecclesiastically compromised in some way. (For more on this last option, see the discussion of Harold II Godwinson's controversial crowning in Chapter 9.) Not all kings secured or required this last status, for reasons that are not always clear. The sources refer to the coronations/consecrations of Æthelred II and Edward the Confessor, but not of Cnut, Harald I Harefoot or Harthacnut.

What is clear is that, with so many 'ingredients' that could go into royal succession, it was possible for not all the 'ingredients' to be included in any given case, and there was plenty of room for complications and false-starts on the progress to the throne. In addition, this does not include the *Realpolitik* that led to Cnut and William of Normandy's highly successful accessions (usurpations?) based on the edge of the sword. Of course, both would claim that this was actually the judgement of heaven in support of their legitimate claim: in Cnut's case his agreement with Edmund Ironside (itself extorted by violent invasion), and in William's case the claim that Edward the Confessor had named him successor in the 1050s and that Harold Godwinson had sworn to support this 'legitimate claim' in 1064.

For Edward the Confessor in 1042, though, things looked good and, despite his long alienation from English politics, a number of the key 'ingredients' were in place. He was undeniably the legitimate son of Æthelred II and Emma of Normandy. He had that crucial royal throneworthiness. In addition, he had been designated as heir by the childless Harthacnut. As if this was not enough, Harthacnut had dispatched his cousin, Svein Estrithson, to Denmark to fight Magnus the Good of Norway and in so doing had pointed towards a division of the Anglo-Danish Empire: Svein Estrithson would have Denmark and Edward the Confessor would have England. However, as we shall see, Svein Estrithson did not accept that this put him out of the running for the crown of England as well. A Viking option was still very much on the table, even if the candidate was currently fighting another Viking ruler for dominance in the northern world of Scandinavia. The consequences of 1016 meant that England was now very closely entangled with the politics of Scandinavia and would continue to remain so until 1066 and, indeed, for the two decades beyond that critical date.

Things in England had been unsettled by the political turmoil and purges of Cnut's reign and by the rollercoaster ride of changing allegiances that the English elites had been forced to embark on during the period 1035–40, when Harald Harefoot and Harthacnut were contesting for the throne. Furthermore, as we have seen, the candidature of Svein Estrithson had not gone away. There *were* decisions to be made in 1042. And decisions were made. The decisive factor in favour of Edward the Confessor's successful accession was the support of Earl Godwin of Wessex. Cnut's 'new man' – the man who had first backed Harthacnut, then got his fingers burnt and so switched to support Harald Harefoot, only to eat humble pie in order to survive on the eventual accession of Harthacnut – decided for Edward. John of Worcester, writing in the 1130s, recorded the tradition that Edward's success was due to the support given him by Godwin. William of Malmesbury, in the 1120s, wrote of Godwin and Archbishop Eadsige of Canterbury acting in concert. Another key player in the support given to Edward, according to John of Worcester, was Lyfing, the Bishop of Worcester, Crediton and Cornwall and a close friend and adviser to Cnut. The *Anglo-Saxon Chronicle* adds that the support of the Londoners also swung behind Edward.

Given the fact that Godwin was uncle to Svein Estrithson and was later to back his campaigns in Denmark, the decision to support Edward so decisively is significant and, perhaps, surprising. Clearly, this shrewd operator had balanced his options and had decided that, of the candidates on offer, it was Edward who was most likely to get the most support within England. Godwin had got it wrong in 1035 (when he had initially declared for Harthacnut against Harald Harefoot) but this time he played his cards more successfully; his was the winning hand in the high-stakes poker of the decisions of 1042.

There is evidence indicating that Godwin was aware of the vulnerability of his position at this moment of regime change. Once more – as when he acted to regain the favour of Harthacnut after earlier backing Harald Harefoot – he offered a fabulously expensive warship, fully kitted out with crew and ornate decoration, to his royal overlord. The record of the gift is found in a document called *Vita Edwardi Regis qui apud West-monasterium Requiescit* (*Life of King Edward who rests at Westminster*). This was compiled in the period 1065–7 and was commissioned by Queen Edith, wife of King Edward the Confessor and daughter of Godwin. The author is unknown, but was a servant of the queen and was probably a Fleming from St Bertin Abbey in St Omer. Despite its title, which suggests that it is a celebration of the life of Edward the Confessor, it was equally geared towards extolling the accomplishments of the Godwin family. Aspects of Book I served the cause of the Godwins, while Book II manipulated aspects of Edward's life to show he was worthy of sainthood – he was eventually canonized in 1161.

The *Vita Edwardi Regis* was the primary source for later biographies of Edward, such as those by Osbert of Clare and Aelred of Rievaulx. Godwin's nautical gift was intended to expunge his past failures and to curry favour in the new political environment. The gift to Harthacnut was in response to Godwin supporting Harthacnut's half-brother, Harald Harefoot; that to Edward was undoubtedly in response to Godwin's role in the arrest, blinding and death of Edward's brother, ætheling Alfred, in 1035–6. Two brothers, two ships; Godwin had a lot of lost ground to make up. There is plenty of evidence that he managed it impressively!

Their decision to back Edward is not explicitly stated in the sources but it is clear from later events that the other senior lay members of the elite must have soon thrown in their lot with Godwin and his allies in backing Edward. Leofric, Earl of Mercia, and Siward, Earl of Northumbria, represented families independent of Godwin and his associates. Leofric was from an established elite family and his father (Leofwine) had served Æthelred II. Siward was, like Godwin, one of the 'new men'. He was a Dane who had been promoted by Cnut and had then married into the Northumbrian aristocracy to secure his position. Their loyalty, added to that of Godwin, secured the throne for Edward. Not for the first time, Mercia and Northumbria acted in alliance; the same would occur in late 1065, but that is getting ahead of our story.

Those who incurred Edward's displeasure were Gunnhildr, the daughter of Cnut's sister and also Emma of Normandy, his own mother. Both were allegedly involved in Scandinavian connections that threatened Edward. A tradition, recorded fifty years later at St Augustine's Abbey in Canterbury, was that Emma was accused of inciting Magnus the Good of Norway to invade England. It was this same Magnus whose invasion of Norway had prevented Harthacnut from returning to England in 1035. In 1042 he was again being resisted in Denmark but this time by Emma's nephew, Svein Estrithson. As we saw in Chapter 6, and will be reminded of in Chapter 9, kings of Norway thought they had a legitimate claim on the English throne due to the tangle of wars, treaties and alliances that drew England into Scandinavian wars and politics as part of the Viking Anglo-Danish Empire.

In this early period of Edward's reign Svein Esthrithson was still a contender for the English throne too. According to Adam of Bremen, Svein claimed that Edward had named him as his heir and it was armed with this status that he had then continued his conflict with Magnus the Good for control of Denmark. Adam recorded this in *Gesta Hammaburgensis Ecclesiae Pontificum (Deeds of the Archbishops of Hamburg)*, also known as *Historia Hammaburgensis Ecclesiae (History of the Church of Hamburg)*. Writing around 1070, Adam claimed that one of his sources for the book was Svein Esthrithson himself, who eventually became King of Denmark in 1047 and ruled it until his death in 1074. Whether Emma was really involved in such a plot is difficult to judge, but Edward moved against her in 1043 and seized her lands and portable wealth. She later experienced some kind of reinstatement, but after 1045 was clearly no longer of influence.

As for Gunnhildr, her banishment in 1044 was at a time of heightened tension between England and Norway since there were rumours that Magnus of Norway – who had temporarily ousted Svein Esthrithson from Denmark – was intending to invade England. Clearly, leading members of Cnut's family were not trusted at such a time of threat.

The Norman presence in Edward's new regime

Normans and other Frenchmen will feature in the history of Edward the Confessor's government, so it is worth exploring just how influential they were from the start: the answer is complex. Edward started his rule with a great deal of continuity from that of the previous reigns. Edward rewarded Godwin for his support by making his son Svein an earl in 1043. Svein Godwinson was only the first to be elevated within this influential family: soon, another of Godwin's sons, Harold, was to be similarly promoted.

In 1042 one of Cnut's loyal supporters, Ordgar, received an estate and in 1044 he was given a second estate by Edward. Looking at the grant of land from 1042 we can see that of the nine thegns (local gentry) who witnessed it, six were Cnut's men and two were loyal supporters of Harthacnut. This was the only charter that survives from 1042 and, similarly, only one survives from 1043 but the pattern is equally striking: of twenty-three thegns, six were the same Cnut's men as in the charter of 1042 and a further nine represented men who had witnessed charters under Harthacnut. Of the ten men who regularly witness charters between 1042 and 1046, seven were Cnut's men,[3] of whom four carried Scandinavian personal names. While this is no sure sign of ethnic origin, it suggests both the presence of Scandinavians at this key social level and also the mixed Anglo-Danish nature of Cnut's following, once he had purged the Anglo-Saxon elite after 1016.

What is interesting is that in this period Normans and other continentals do not feature highly among such people. Some of Edward's followers who accompanied him from Normandy are certainly there, and we can identify the clerks, Leofric and Herman, from 1041 onwards, but as yet there is no sign of Robert of Jumièges or Ralph of Mantes, both of whom would later play important roles. This suggests that it took time for Norman and French influence to grow. Robert of Jumièges finally appears among the list of bishops in 1046, having been appointed Bishop of London in 1044. From there his rise was meteoric, becoming Archbishop of Canterbury in 1051 (a post he held until being deposed and forced into exile in 1052).

It seems that the early 1050s saw the turning point in continental influence, for it was in 1050 that Ralph of Mantes (a Frenchman) first appeared in the witness lists. Other continentals, particularly Normans, were also influential from this period onwards. Bishop William of London (William 'the Norman') and Ulf of Dorchester (also referred to as 'Ulfus Normanus') were major players in the crisis of 1051–2 (when Godwin was exiled and then returned) and there was a 'Norman colony' in Herefordshire in the 1050s. It was here that the Norman knight, Osbern Pentecost, built the castle at Ewyas, under the patronage of Ralph of Mantes. The Norman knight, Richard fitz Scrob, similarly built Richard's Castle on the border of Herefordshire and Shropshire some time before 1051. In addition, Robert fitz Wimarc was a leading figure at court and attended the king at his deathbed. Robert fitz Wimarc was related to Duke William of Normandy as well as to King Edward of England, although his byname suggests a Breton connection in his ancestry, since 'Wimarc' was a form of the Breton name Wiomar'ch. This Norman and French influence was, therefore, apparent within the court of Edward the Confessor and this can be seen as a factor leading to the events of 1066.[4]

The high water mark of this Norman influence seems to have occurred in 1051–2 when Godwin overplayed his hand and it finally looked as if Edward could free himself from an unwanted and over-mighty subject.

Happy families?

On 23 January 1045, King Edward married Edith, the daughter of Earl Godwin. According to the *Vita Edwardi Regis* she was also anointed and crowned as queen. It is likely that this indeed occurred and would have secured the position of the Godwin family at the top of Anglo-Saxon society. But how happy was Edward with this situation? The evidence indicates that it was a relationship that hid a great many tensions beneath the surface.

By the time that Edward became king, the houses of Godwin of Wessex and, to a lesser extent, that of Leofric of Mercia had created for themselves positions of enormous power within Anglo-Saxon society; as we have seen this had developed under Cnut. This was a position that the newly arrived Edward found difficult to successfully challenge.

Edward's marriage to Edith greatly increased the power of the house of Godwin and it is difficult to be certain how much choice Edward had in the matter. There is every likelihood that this was a marriage alliance that even a king could not refuse. Given his speed in parting from her in 1051, we must question just how much choice Edward felt that he had had in agreeing to the marriage in the first place.

The behaviour of the Godwins caused problems in surprising and shocking ways. In 1046 Godwin's eldest son, Svein, abducted the Abbess of Leominster and for this crime was exiled in 1047. In exile he travelled to Flanders and Denmark, from where he was expelled for some unspecified crime (which adds to the impression we get of a violent and criminally out of control young man). On his return, in 1049, his brother Harold and cousin Beorn refused to give up Svein's lands that had been given to them in his absence. So Svein was denied the right to return but did so anyway and, accompanied by his cousin Beorn, made as if to visit the king. On the way, though, Svein murdered Beorn. Svein was then declared *nithing* (Old English for 'nothing', 'utterly outlawed') by the men of the royal fleet. But still he returned in 1050. He was pardoned by the king and regained his earldom.

Edward's role in all this was complex. He appears to have protected Svein, as later he would attempt to protect another (slightly less maverick) of Godwin's sons, Tostig, in 1065. Why ever would he do such a thing? Svein was clearly out of control. The answer may be that in both cases it was Harold Godwinson who was involved in the opposition to an out-of-control brother. And Harold Godwinson, even as early as 1049, was already a very powerful man. He was already Earl of East Anglia (something of a super-earldom) and Edward may have feared that here was another Godwin in the making! This illustrates just what a problem Edward faced with regard to the Godwin family.

The episode of Svein Godwinson raises an uncomfortable question as to how we should view the Godwin family. There is a tendency to view them as the patriotic English and Edward the Confessor as an ineffective king who opened the door to foreign influences, most notably the Normans; Harold Godwinson's death at Hastings only adds to the romantic impression of heroic defenders of English interests against foreign aggressors. At the time though, and certainly in the 1040s and 1050s, things may have appeared rather differently. King Edward may well have agreed with the view of Eric John that the Godwins were 'a cancer on the body politic that had to be cut out'.[5] The Godwins continue to divide historians and it has been argued that, difficult as they were to manage, King Edward still succeeded in keeping control and his weakness should not be exaggerated.[6] What is undeniable is that managing the Godwins *was* a challenge.

Edward's feelings towards these over-mighty subjects can clearly be seen in the events of the next years, 1050 and 1051. In 1050 the Norman, Robert of Jumièges, was made Archbishop of Canterbury by King Edward in the face of opposition by Godwin who backed a kinsman for the post. Godwin was furious and attacked the estates of Christ Church Canterbury (or perhaps just those of the archbishop), but had to accept he had lost. By way of compensation, his ally Abbot Spearhafoc of Abingdon was made Bishop of London by the king. Robert of Jumièges travelled to Rome to collect his *pallium* (the ceremonial scarf of office) and, on the journey, probably took an offer of the English crown from Edward to Duke William of Normandy. The later Norman chronicler William of Poitiers, writing his *Gesta Guillelmi* (*The Deeds of William*) in the 1070s, claimed as much. On his return the new archbishop announced that Spearhafoc was not suitable to the bishop's post. In addition, a new abbot was appointed to Abingdon who was related to the king and a Norman was made Bishop of London. It looked like game, set and match to King Edward and his Norman allies. It would be interesting to know what Godwin said. But it was about to get worse for the Earl of Wessex.

In 1051, King Edward's brother-in-law, Eustace, Count of Boulogne, had a violent encounter in Kent with the people of the strategically sited port of Dover. Godwin, as the Earl of Wessex, was ordered to severely punish the people of Dover. This put him in a very difficult position. On one hand he had been given a direct commission by his king. On the other hand Dover was very much in his sphere of influence; it was one of his towns. And it seems clear that in this conflict between English and foreigners, Godwin's sympathies lay with the people of Dover. As a result he refused to attack and punish the town and so disobeyed the orders of his king.

This led to the exile not only of Godwin but also of Godwin's sons. Even the disaffected Svein stood by the rest of his family, prompting the biting comment on the Godwins that he had 'remembered the adage the family that slays together stays together'.[7] Godwin family unity was therefore maintained at this critical point in time. Svein died during this exile, in 1052, while returning from pilgrimage to Jerusalem. Godwin went into (temporary) exile with his ally the Count of Flanders. It was probably at this time that Godwin's son Tostig married Judith, the half-sister of Count Baldwin of Flanders. At the same time as exiling the male members of the Godwin family, Edward sent his wife, Edith, to a nunnery.

Just what was going on in this crisis? There is a possibility that there was an unintended spiral into conflict, king and earl finding themselves in irreconcilable positions. Edward could not ignore the slight to his continental relative, while Godwin could not bring himself to punish one of his own towns where he had a strong personal following and support. On the other hand it has all the stuff of conspiracy about it: an explosive situation is engineered between over-confident foreigners and locals in a sensitive spot; a crisis duly occurs; Godwin is put in an impossible position; the king finally has the opportunity to expunge the entire Godwin clan and free himself from an unwanted marriage at the same time. In one decisive action Edward the Confessor could remove the most troubling feature of Cnut's legacy – the Godwins – and install his own men in their place.

The events of this year are described in detail in the *Vita Edwardi Regis*. Given that this was commissioned by Godwin's daughter after Edward the Confessor's death and as she was the sister of the man who, in January 1066, became King Harold II Godwinson, it is not surprising that the text is often favourable to the house of Godwin. It tells us that the exiled Earl Godwin sent to Edward to ask for peace but that 'the malice of evil men had shut up the merciful ears of the king'. The writer of the *Vita Edwardi Regis* wanted readers to share his outrage at the way in which Edward was being manipulated by those who opposed Godwin and had no care for justice or what was good for the king and the kingdom. We might, though, see a very different reality behind these words. It rather looks as if the king was glad to be finally rid of Godwin and was enjoying the absence of this troublesome subject.[8]

If so, the king's triumph was short-lived, for he could not enforce the exile of Godwin and his family. By 1052, Edward had been forced to restore Godwin's earldom to him. As manuscript C of the *Chronicle* records, this was 'unconditionally and as fully and completely as he had ever held it, and all his sons all that they had held before.'[9] This amounted to a complete climb-down by Edward. He had struck at Godwin but failed to land the killer blow. Now it was his turn to back down in the face of a family that was too strong to crush and an Anglo-Saxon elite that would not back the king to the point of civil war. This speaks well of Anglo-Saxon civic maturity and political responsibility, but one can imagine that Edward the Confessor would have described it rather differently. Edith was restored to her position at the king's side and to the royal bed at the same time. It was a family reunion that one can only wince to imagine.

A situation that Cnut had created of powerful but insecure elites had evolved into a new phase, for under Edward these same elites were now impossible to suppress. This was a direct result of the kind of government created by Cnut, as he purged the old elites and built up a new cadre of supporters. This was now acting in combination with the consequences of the exile of Edward that Cnut's conquest had also directly caused.

Those foreign supporters of Edward who had helped engineer the Godwin fall – including Robert of Jumièges, Archbishop of Canterbury, and the Norman bishop, Ulf – fled. Frenchmen holding land in Herefordshire fled to Scotland. It is likely that it was at this point that Robert of Jumièges took with him younger members of the Godwin clan – a young son named Wulfnoth and Svein's son, named Hakon – who had been surrendered to the king as hostages prior to Godwin being forced into exile. These forgotten Godwins would briefly resurface in 1064 when Harold Godwinson's apparent attempt to secure their release backfired spectacularly, with consequences of historic proportions.

Living with 'the enemy'?

With the Godwins back, their power went from strength to strength. Harold became Earl of Wessex in 1053, on the death of his father; eventually his brother Gyrth received the earldom of East Anglia; his brother Leofwine gained Middlesex; his brother Tostig gained Northumbria. The Godwin family dominated England. The only powerful earldom that lay outside Godwinson control was Mercia, which remained in the control of the family of Leofric (his son Ælfgar briefly gained East Anglia, but lost it to Gyrth Godwinson in 1055). This was a situation allowed by Edward, but whether from choice or not is not clear. It all seemed a long way from the attempt to exile and neutralize the Godwin family in 1051–2.

However, one thing eluded the Godwins: a royal child born from the marriage of Queen Edith Godwinsdaughter and King Edward. The lack of an heir can be explained by many things, biological and relational. At a distance of over a millennium we cannot now diagnose the cause of the childlessness of Edith and Edward. In Edward's old age or shortly after his death the writer of the *Vita Edwardi Regis* claimed that Edward lived a celibate life with Edith due to his religious determination to remain a virgin; this was the start of Edward the Confessor's journey to sainthood and the theme was taken up by Osbert of Clare in 1138 as part of a campaign for Edward's canonization. At first glance this may seem a predictable strategy by both the writer of the *Vita Edwardi* and by Osbert. The lack of an heir was a major problem and a failure of kingship, but not if it arose from a decision based on holiness rather than an inability to have children.

There is, though, the real possibility that Edward's lack of an heir stemmed from a deliberate decision to deny the Godwins a royal succession. Writing in 1125 (and so earlier than Osbert of Clare), William of Malmesbury, in his *Gesta regum Anglorum* (*Deeds of the Kings of the English*), speculated concerning the king's alleged chastity: 'But whether he did this because of his hatred of her family (which he widely dissimulated at the time) or because of his love of chastity, I really do not know.'[10] If the former, then it was Edward's final act of defiance in the face of the domination of the Godwins. It would be consistent both with Svein Esthrithson's claim that he had been promised the throne, even over any son born to Edward and with the 'Norman Strategy' that seems to have emerged by the early 1050s. What was clear was that there was no heir and something needed to be done regarding the succession.

Succession strategies ... the 'Viking Connection' again

Despite Edward the Confessor's securing of the throne, the Viking threat had never gone away. A charter dating from 1044 and granting land at Pitminster in Somerset to the church at Old Minster, Winchester, indicates that Edward feared for the peace of England.[11] In its *proem* (introduction) the scribe describes how Edward is 'not without anxiety for the peace of the land we have acquired...'.[12] The threat was from Scandinavia.

Between 1044 and his death in 1047, Magnus the Good of Norway also ruled Denmark and appears to have entertained plans to invade England. According to a late tradition, recorded at St Albans Abbey in a mixed source – parts of which date from the first half of the thirteenth century and parts from the late thirteenth/early fourteenth century – early in the reign of Edward the Confessor there was a serious threat of invasion from Denmark. If successful, this would have made Magnus the Good the ruler of Norway, Denmark and England: an empire comparable to that forged by Cnut the Great. Magnus the Good was in a strong position as he had just secured (in 1043) a massive victory over the Wends, a Slavic confederation of the southern Baltic. The *Chronicle*, though, states that Magnus was prevented from invading due to his warfare with Svein Estrithson in Denmark, while the Icelandic source *Heimskringla* (*Circle of the World*), compiled in Iceland by Snorri Sturluson in c.1225–30, claims that Edward wrote a letter begging the Norwegian king not to invade! This is clearly legendary and from a much later source than the *Chronicle*.

Godwin was also involved in this complicated manoeuvring, advising Edward to send assistance to Svein Estrithson, who had been Magnus the Good's deputy in Denmark but had later attempted to break free from Magnus' overlordship in 1045. Magnus was the greater threat to England, and the longer he could be kept embroiled in a northern war with Svein Estrithson, the better. This kept both Norwegian and Danish

Viking fleets away from England. However, Edward opted for a policy of neutrality and the eventual result was that Magnus prevailed over Svein Estrithson, but then died in 1047.[13] This then raised the possibility of an intervention in England by Svein Estrithson (King of Denmark 1047–74) since he was no longer threatened by Magnus.[14] Svein Estrithson turned his mind to his own invasion of England but was prevented from implementing his plan because he soon faced renewed war with Norway, under Magnus the Good's successor, Harald Hardrada.

The threat from Scandinavia, coupled with his lack of an heir and the feud with the Godwins, initiated a succession crisis that dominated the last ten years of Edward's reign. In response he adopted a successive series of strategies to attempt to solve the problem.

There may have been a brief 'Svein Estrithson Strategy' in the early 1040s, since Svein clearly believed he had been promised the English crown by Edward the Confessor[15] and Adam of Bremen recorded the tradition in about 1070.

Then there was the 'Norman Strategy'. During 1051 (or 1052) manuscript *D* of the *Chronicle* (also John of Worcester) says that William of Normandy visited England. It is not clear why. The visit was possibly linked to later Norman claims that Edward promised William the English crown. There is a real possibility that the visit was in response to a promise of the crown that had been carried to Normandy by Robert of Jumièges in 1050 – the dates certainly fit very neatly. There is no clear answer to this but, given the fact that the visit occurred during the exile of the Godwins, there is a real likelihood that Edward was finally trying to settle the succession crisis and felt bold enough to adopt a 'Norman Strategy' in the absence of Godwin and his sons. It was also part of an anti-Viking strategy, which once more reminds us of the Viking dimension in English politics in the eleventh century.

The *Chronicle* says of William's visit that '*se cyning hine underfeng*' ('the king received him'). The Old English word *underfeng* carried connotations of 'received as a vassal': clearly, William of Normandy accepted the lordship of King Edward. It was not just a family visit, nor that merely of a man who had been promised the crown: Edward the Confessor expected something in return. And that was almost certainly the closing of Norman ports to Viking fleets.[16] In the context of the time, with rulers in Norway and Denmark claiming their right to the English throne, it was an astute move. Moreover, it was consistent with Anglo-Saxon policy that stretched back half a century. The same need to secure both sides of the English Channel against Scandinavian marauders that had prompted Æthelred II's marriage to Emma of Normandy in 1002 and Cnut's marriage to the same woman in 1017, now drove Edward the Confessor to offer the English crown to Duke William and demand his loyalty in return. It had the further advantage of sidelining the

Godwin family. The return of Godwin and sons in 1052 put an end to this 'Norman Strategy' – but not in the mind of Duke William of Normandy.

This was then followed by what we might call the 'Edward the Exile Strategy'. This led by a circuitous route to Hungary and back again, a route that had been decided by Cnut forty years before. As we saw in Chapter 7, Edward the Exile and his son Edgar Ætheling were recalled to England in 1057. If the 'Norman Strategy' was no longer viable with the ascendancy of the Godwinsons, then this was a strong alternative. Edward the Exile, although unconnected to English politics, nevertheless had an impeccable royal claim to the throne. This was not the only factor necessary, but it was the primary one. The 'Edward the Exile Strategy' seemed a strong runner, yet it fell at the first hurdle because within days of his arrival Edward the Exile was dead. The manuscript *D* of the *Chronicle* records the shocking event:

> We do not know for what reason it was brought about that he was not allowed to see [the face?] of his kinsman, King Edward. Alas, that was a miserable fate and grievous to all this people that he so speedily ended his life after he came to England, to the misfortune of this poor people.[17]

Medieval people could die suddenly. In an age before germ theory and antibiotics, an infection could swiftly lead to death. Edward the Exile was not the first person to die suddenly without any discernible reason. However, his death sounds highly suspicious. Was this a Godwinson conspiracy? There is no evidence to support this accusation but, suffice it to say that a royal with a strong claim to the throne had died as soon as he arrived in England leaving a son who was only about five years of age.

In that same year died both Earl Leofric of Mercia (to be replaced as earl by his son Ælfgar) and Ralph of Mantes, Earl of Hereford between 1051 and 1057. An established non-Godwin and a Frenchman with – as the son of Edward the Confessor's sister Godgifu – an outside claim to the English throne had both exited the political stage. There is no hint of suspicion in either case – and Ralph seems to have been on good terms with the Godwinsons – but the turn of these events greatly strengthened the position of the Godwin family. Harold Godwinson had the earldom of Hereford added to his already impressive portfolio and may actually have been given it as early as 1055, following Ralph's defeat at the hands of the Welsh. It may be noted that, in terms of Edward the Confessor's closest family members, the number shrank yet further in 1064 when Earl Ralph's brother Walter III Count of Mantes died.[18]

The 'Edward the Exile Strategy' had collapsed. It could perhaps, in time, be replaced by an 'Edgar Ætheling Strategy', but it would be years before the young son of Edward the Exile would be a viable candidate in an age of competing claims by experienced practitioners of violence. So, unsurprisingly, it was not Edgar Ætheling but Harold Godwinson who succeeded Edward the Confessor in January 1066.

How to make sense of all of this? It is possible that the sequence was: the 'Norman strategy' to block the exiled Godwins; then the 'Edward the Exile strategy' to block the returned Godwins who would not accept William but would find it hard to oppose Edward the Exile. This may even have been encouraged by Queen Edith, who may have seen the succession passing to Edgar Ætheling under the political oversight of herself and her brothers Harold and Tostig. The giving of the title 'Ætheling' by the king clearly signals that Edgar was considered throne-worthy and his royal connection was impeccable. In the early twelfth century, William of Malmesbury reported a tradition that King Edward at one point nominated Edgar as his heir. A document called the *Liber Vitae* (*Book of Life*), from New Minster, Winchester, which was compiled from 1031 onwards as a list of names of brethren and benefactors, names him as *clito* or heir. His position, though, was not strong since his father had never been crowned (the usual route to status as an ætheling) and he possessed neither land nor retainers at the court of Edward the Confessor.

Then finally, in January 1066, there was the 'Godwin strategy' and the designation of Harold Godwinson as the only person able to hold the political situation together in the very different circumstances of January 1066, with his brother Tostig exiled (as detailed below), and Harald Hardrada of Norway, Svein Estrithson of Denmark and William of Normandy all pressing claims to the throne. By this time Harold was a virtual sub-king; Edward the Confessor may even have come to accept that he held this status, though it was never officially stated.

Harold Godwinson and 'that oath'

In 1064 occurred something that is uniformly ignored by the Anglo-Saxon sources but which plays a major part in the Norman written sources and on the Bayeux Tapestry: Harold journeyed to the continent and landed in northern France. There are a number of options for why Harold went: it was an accident and his ship was blown off course (found as a later tradition in William of Malmesbury); he was negotiating an otherwise unknown marriage alliance; he was going to negotiate the return of the two Godwin hostages taken to Normandy by Robert of Jumièges in 1052 – his younger brother Wulfnoth and his nephew Hakon (Svein Godwinson's son). If the latter, and this seems the most likely explanation, then it was yet another unintended consequence of the 'Norman Connection' that characterized the rule of Edward the Confessor. Although the Bayeux Tapestry presents the event as a mission designed to promise the crown to Duke William, it may really have been a private enterprise trip, without royal sanction. The Bayeux Tapestry offers a Norman view on events, but the particular scene illustrating Harold's eventual return looks very much like he is being admonished by King Edward. This may, of course, be reading too much into the scene, but it is possible that Harold took himself to the continent in an attempt to free his relatives, got into difficulties (as we shall see) and was criticized on his return, and later Norman sources turned the whole episode into an official mission designed to assure William of his right to the English throne with Harold's sworn support.

In the event, Harold appears to have been shipwrecked. There he was arrested by Count Guy of Ponthieu and then 'rescued' by William. As William's honoured guest he accompanied the Norman knights in an attack on Brittany, and was honoured with armour and weapons. And at this point things started to go horribly wrong from Harold's perspective: it seems that William probably regarded this event as a knighting ceremony and thought that Harold was now 'his man'. We can be sure that Harold regarded it as no such thing.

Norman sources assert that, before leaving, Harold swore an oath of loyalty to William. The Bayeux Tapestry dramatically recalls the scene. He probably did so, although the English sources are silent. From this would come the Norman accusation of perjury and oath-breaking. Harold may well have argued that it was given under duress and was not valid; we simply do not know.

Mid-winter crisis, 1065–66

We have seen how, despite the centralized nature of the late Anglo-Saxon state, a powerful strata of earls had been inherited from Cnut. To be fair, this was not just due to him since Æthelred II had struggled to control powerful subjects whose regional powerbases were hard to challenge and whose loyalty could be suspect, indeed at times treacherous. This power of the English earls, compared with that of the king, can also be seen in the revolt against Tostig Godwinson that occurred in late 1065. Tostig was a younger son of Godwin and seems to have been Edward's favourite member of the house of Godwin; he had been made Earl of Northumbria following the death of Siward in 1055.

The choice of Tostig was a questionable one for, while he ruled his earldom for some years, he never seems to have been popular. The situation came to a head in 1065. It was then that the thegns of Yorkshire descended on York, expelled Tostig and sent instead for Morcar, who was a member of the house of Leofric of Mercia. Not for the first time, Northumbria and Mercia were acting in concert. With Morcar's elevation a rival house to that of the Godwins controlled the Midlands and the North. Morcar's elder brother, Edwin, was son of Ælfgar, the previous Earl of Mercia, and grandson of Leofric, who had also been Earl of Mercia. Edwin succeeded to his father's title when Ælfgar died in 1062. Now his younger brother, Morcar, had become Earl of Northumbria.

The ailing Edward favoured Tostig in this crisis but he was powerless in the face of a Northumbrian and Mercian elite conspiracy against Tostig: as a result, he was forced to dismiss Tostig in favour of Morcar.[19] In an act of civic responsibility, Harold Godwinson refused to back his brother and tip the country into civil war. In so doing he earned Tostig's bitter resentment. Going into exile, Tostig was determined to cause as much trouble as possible, and his bitterness led him to support Harald Hardrada of Norway's bid for the English throne in September 1066.

The death of Edward the Confessor

In November 1065 King Edward's health began to fail. It was the start of a sudden and short crisis: on 5 January 1066, Edward the Confessor died and Harold was crowned the next day, immediately after Edward's funeral. In December 2005 Edward the Confessor's tomb was finally found, one thousand years after his birth. The ancient site was located underneath Westminster Abbey. The location of the tomb had been a mystery to archaeologists until ground-penetrating radar technology revealed its location.[20]

The *Vita Edwardi Regis* claims that Edward had nominated Harold on his deathbed. A similar scene (but with no explanation of recommendation of course) can be seen on the Bayeux Tapestry. All three manuscripts of the *Chronicle* agree that Edward nominated Harold. Even the Norman chronicler, William of Poitiers, accepted that Edward did this. He may well have done so, having reconsidered and abandoned the earlier nomination of William. It was the first and only recorded attempt by an English non-royal noble to take the throne: with the exceptions of Svein Forkbeard and Cnut, no-one outside of the dynasty of Alfred the Great had held the English kingship since the 870s. And Harold II Godwinson would not hold it for long. It was just the start of 1066 and it would be a momentous year.

CHAPTER 9

1066: The Viking Year?

When Edward the Confessor died, it was Harold Godwinson, a non-royal, who took the throne as King Harold II. As we have already seen, it was the unintended fall-out from the Viking Conquest of 1016 that had made this unprecedented promotion possible. However, the Viking involvement did not end there. Predictably – as a result of the Göta River Agreement of 1040, made between Harthacnut and Magnus the Good of Norway – the Viking king of Norway, Harald Hardrada, was drawn into the contested succession for the crown of England and it was his invasion in September that so wrong-footed Harold Godwinson as to cost him the Battle of Hastings on 14 October 1066. But, first, the events of that momentous year prior to Hastings require our attention.

A stitch in time ... the Bayeux Tapestry

One of our best sources for the events of 1066 is not the usual written source in the form of a chronicle or a history but perhaps the world's most famous tapestry – the Bayeux Tapestry. The tapestry is over 70 metres long and, although it is called a tapestry, it is in fact an embroidery that is stitched, in coloured woollen yarns on linen. (In contrast, a tapestry is traditionally woven *into* cloth on a vertical loom.)

The tapestry is first recorded in 1476, in an inventory of Bayeux Cathedral. However, the style indicates that it is late eleventh-century in date. In France legend has it that it was made by William's queen, Matilda of Flanders and her ladies-in-waiting. For that reason, in France it is sometimes known as *La Tapisserie de la Reine Mathilde* ('The Tapestry of Queen Matilda'). Most modern experts believe that the Bayeux Tapestry was probably commissioned in the 1070s, by Bishop Odo of Bayeux, who was the half-brother of William the Conqueror. It was, though, almost certainly stitched by English craftswomen, possibly in Odo's power base in Kent. Anglo-Saxon seamstresses were famous for high-quality embroidery work of this kind.

The value of the tapestry is that, for the first time in *English* history, we have a dramatic narrative pictorially representing the events of the past. It is, in effect, a graphic novel version of the end of Anglo-Saxon England. As such, it depicts the events leading up to 1066, starting with Harold's ill-fated visit to Normandy in 1064 and culminating in the dramatic events of the Battle of Hastings in 1066. The original tapestry is on display at Bayeux.

Despite the occasional suggestions that Anglo-Saxon Kentish embroiderers stitched critical and subversive messages into aspects of the pictures and text, the clear reality is that this is evidence as seen through the eyes of the victorious Normans, even if executed via the skilled fingers of Kentish embroiderers.

Witnesses for the defence and the prosecution

The accounts of what happened in 1066 vary widely depending on the agenda of their author. Consequently, there is no such thing as a surviving balanced account. Some defend Harold, while others criticize him for taking the throne. Some of these 'witnesses' will appear in this chapter, so it will help to give a very brief overview of their take on the events.

We see things from the Anglo-Saxon side in the annals of the *Anglo-Saxon Chronicle*. We also see accounts that sometimes allow some insight into English outlooks from a later generation of Anglo-Norman historians writing in England. These include John of Worcester, in his *Chronicon ex Chronicis* (*Chronicle of other Chronicles*), completed shortly after 1140, and Henry of Huntingdon's *Historia Anglorum* (*History of the English*), written c.1125 to 1154.

We hear the Norman view in: the *Carmen de Hastingae Proelio* (*Song of the Battle of Hastings*), probably written by Bishop Guy of Amiens as early as early 1067 and certainly by 1068; William of Jumièges' *Gesta Normannorum Ducum* (*Deeds of the Norman Dukes*), written shortly before 1060 and extended early in 1070 at the Conqueror's request to include an account of the Conquest; and William of Poitiers' *Gesta Guillelmi* (*The Deeds of William*), probably written by c.1077. In addition, there is Orderic Vitalis' *Historia Ecclesiastica* (the *History of the Church*), which was written in Normandy, between 1114 and 1141. Finally, there is the voice of Wace, in his *Roman de Rou* (*Story of Rollo*), a verse history of the dukes of Normandy from the time of the Viking Rollo of Normandy to the battle of Tinchebray, in 1106. Started in 1160, it was completed in the mid-1170s. Of these the *Carmen*, though Norman in outlook, is less partisan than some of the other Norman-oriented sources.

Harold Godwinson's accession

As we have seen in the previous chapter, Harold acceded to the throne on the death of Edward the Confessor. Harold had been promised the throne by King Edward, a point explicitly stated in manuscript *E* of the

Anglo-Saxon Chronicle and the *Vita Ædwardi Regis*, which are both pro-Godwin sources of information. However, Duke William was convinced that he was the true heir in keeping with Norman legal custom, which stressed the promise made by Edward the Confessor and the oath sworn by Harold Godwinson while in Normandy. In direct competition to both Harold and William was Svein Estrithson of Denmark. In the face of this Viking claim the later Norman historian, William of Poitiers, made the unlikely assertion that Svein accepted the superiority of William's right to the throne.[1] Then, of course, there was Harald Hardrada of Norway.

Life was getting complicated. As a result of Cnut's Viking Conquest in 1016, Harthacnut's diplomacy and Edward the Confessor's indecision after 1042, there were two Viking kings (of Denmark and Norway), one Norman duke and an Anglo-Danish earl who all thought that they had a legitimate claim to the throne of England as 1066 dawned. This meant that Harold's succession was far from clear-cut, and 1066 would prove to an interesting and dramatic year.

It is easy to present Harold Godwinson's taking of the throne as a coup. However, things were more complex than that. When Edward died, on 5 January 1066, the thirty-nine leading noblemen who were present at Edward's Christmas court and who then accepted and then acclaimed Harold Godwinson as their king (he was rapidly crowned on 6 January) were thoroughly representative of the regions and ethnicities that made up late Anglo-Saxon England. As such, they stood for various elite voices of the land and they included foreign as well as native members of the English nobility. This means that the decision can be viewed as the voice of the political nation as it existed in the mid-eleventh century.[2]

So therefore – whatever we make of tangled and questionable Scandinavian diplomacy, Edward's earlier competing succession strategies, Harold's oath and William's expectations – Harold's final nomination by Edward and acclamation by the leading nobles was legal, although unprecedented.[3] The setting aside of Edgar Ætheling, with his impeccable royal bloodline, was problematic, but his legitimacy could not outweigh all that lay in Harold Godwinson's side of the political scales. His youth and his lack of an English power-base greatly weakened his candidature. Under the gathering clouds of January 1066, with the likelihood of one Norman and two Viking invasion fleets soon to be prepared, the decision to back Harold was both understandable and justifiable.

Harold's coronation is depicted in the Bayeux Tapestry. It is likely to have taken place in Westminster Abbey – the first of many coronations to take place there – given that it took place directly after Edward's burial there.[4] There is some discrepancy in the sources about who crowned Harold, with the English sources claiming the ceremony was performed by Ealdred, Archbishop of York, while the Norman sources claim it was

Stigand, Archbishop of Canterbury. Stigand was a controversial figure who was excommunicated by several popes for his pluralism in holding the two bishoprics of Canterbury and Winchester at the same time. His appointment as Archbishop of Canterbury had not been recognized by the pope and, therefore, Stigand had gained his archbishopric uncanonically and he did not hold a valid *pallium*. Given this, it is highly unlikely that Stigand did crown Harold, as Harold would have been acutely aware of the implications of this on the legitimacy of his coronation. The Normans would also have been aware of this and it is likely that they deliberately refer to Stigand in order to undermine the legitimacy of Harold and highlight the rightful kingship of William. It is important to note that Stigand was not in the practice of consecrating bishops – he only consecrated two and that was in the brief period when he held a legitimate *pallium* – and Ealdred of York usually took on these duties, so it would be highly strange for Stigand rather than Ealdred to have crowned Harold.

One of Harold's first tasks was to ensure support from the whole of his kingdom. Despite the fact that England had been a largely united kingdom for over a hundred years there were still significant divisions between the north and south, and the earls of the north were very powerful actors. In addition to this, the influx of Scandinavian settlers in the late ninth century had further differentiated the east and north, and the tenth-century Viking kingdom of York had underscored the sense of northern distinction. As part of his unifying campaign, Harold travelled with Bishop Wulfstan of Worchester north to meet with Edwin, Earl of Mercia and Morcar, Earl of Northumbria. During 1066 Harold married Edwin and Morcar's sister, Edith, and it is very possible that this marriage took place at the beginning of 1066 during this conciliatory visit. This marriage replaced his earlier 'Danish marriage' with yet another Edith, Edith Swan-neck. Harold already had grown-up children by Edith Swan-neck, but this marriage was set aside to be replaced by the political marriage to Edwin and Morcar's sister: an alliance that secured the loyalty of the Midlands and the North. There are echoes in this of the two marriages contracted by Cnut to Ælfgifu of Northampton and Emma of Normandy earlier in the century. It is also likely that the visit included a promise from Harold that his brother Tostig would not be permitted to return to his Northumbrian earldom.[5]

Spring 1066: Tostig makes his move

The *Chronicle* tells us that Harold returned from York in time to celebrate Easter in Westminster on 16 April. On 24 April Halley's Comet appeared in the skies and seems to have been unusually bright. Such celestial apparitions were commonly thought to foretell disaster and in later sources it is often connected to the fall of Harold. How people viewed it at the time is hard to decide, but the long-haired-star that appears on the Bayeux Tapestry indicates that the Normans, at least, later thought that its appearance was significant.

Shortly afterwards, in May 1066, Tostig made his first, abortive, attempt to invade England. Tostig, as we have seen, was Harold's younger brother who had previously been Earl of Northumbria before being deposed and outlawed in 1065. Tostig landed in the Isle of Wight with a fleet provided by his brother-in-law, the Count of Flanders. There is also evidence that he had recruited Orkney Vikings to join his enterprise. He then raided along the coast until he reached Sandwich. Harold was in London when he heard the news of his brother's attacks and called out the fyrd – the army of English free farmers obliged to fight for their king when required to do so. Combined with the household troops of the king and the household troops of local nobles this made a formidable force, and we should not think of it as simply made up of armed rustics. Faced with an army led by his brother and given the very limited success he had had in the south, he fled north.

Tostig made an unsuccessful attempt to recruit his brother Gyrth to his cause and he then proceeded to attack Lincolnshire. Edwin and Morcar were ready for him and led an army into Lincolnshire, decisively beating Tostig and sending him packing to Malcolm, King of Scots. There he would remain throughout the summer, licking his wounds and plotting his next move.

Summer 1066: anti-climax

Tostig's actions demonstrated that the conditions were now favourable for a channel crossing and, aware of the intentions of William of Normandy, Harold seems to have kept the fyrd mustered to deal with a Norman invasion of the South Coast. However, this invasion was not to be forthcoming. Instead, William watched, and he waited, and he made his meticulous preparations. These included the gathering of all the great magnates of Normandy, called to attend the dedication of his wife Matilda's new abbey at St Etienne, in Caen, on 18 June 1066. There William asked for the blessing of God on his invasion.

In July, William's invasion fleet moved north from Dives to St Valery sur Somme, but still it did not cross the Channel. The sources say that their leader was waiting for fair weather, but he may equally have been awaiting news that Tostig had made his move in the north. Either way, it was a perfect strategy. The fyrd was a levy of farmers, who by August were clamouring to be released so that they could take in their harvest. At the beginning of September, Harold had no option but to let them go – they had, after all, by now been on standby for four months. Harold disbanded his troops on 8 September, as provisions had been consumed, and returned to London. The Anglo-Saxon fleet lost many ships to a storm on its way to London; there is a possibility that, before this occurred, Harold had ordered a naval foray against William, which forced the Normans back at this point. This is uncertain but there is a hint of it in manuscript E of the *Chronicle*.

With summer gone and autumn approaching, bringing with it unfavourable weather and autumn storms, Harold must have thought that the chances of invasion were diminishing by the day. While Svein Estrithson had not moved, Harold must have been aware of there being some kind of threat posed by Harald Hardrada, in addition to that from Normandy. However it was the Normans who seemed the greatest danger. But it looked like the worst had passed: Harold had held his throne in the face of competition from north and east. A real threat from Normandy and a vague threat from Scandinavia had not led to conflict.

Autumn 1066: the Norwegian invasion

Unfortunately for Harold, his troubles were only just beginning. Despite Tostig's resounding defeat earlier in the year, he was by no means broken and so ended his summer in Scotland identifying suitable partners for a further invasion. He found one in the form of Harald Hardrada, King of Norway, a seasoned warrior and in possession of a tenuous claim to the English throne. In September 1066, Harald Hardrada made his move.[6] This invasion seems to have come as a complete surprise to the English, which would suggest this was not part of a longstanding invasion plan but rather one engineered by Tostig during his exile in Scotland.[7]

Harald Hardrada was in need of money and victory. On becoming king of Norway he had failed in an expensive and long war to gain the throne of Denmark too: by 1064 this attempt had ended in an inconclusive treaty with King Svein Esthrithson (who had returned to Denmark following the death of Magnus of Norway). Harald Hardrada was left poorer and without a victory. England offered the possibility of renewed Viking expansion, and he seized his opportunity.

Harald Hardrada set sail from Norway in September, meeting Tostig's small force along the way and arriving in the Humber estuary; later Norse sources claimed he led 300 ships. After landing on English soil, Harald led his troops towards York where he was met just outside the city by the combined forces of Earl Edwin of Mercia and Earl Morcar of Northumbria. The Battle of Gate Fulford took place on 20 September; it seems to have been long and bloody, with heavy casualties on both sides. Edwin and Morcar were inexperienced military leaders facing a seasoned warrior who had once been a member of the Varangian Guard, an elite unit in the Byzantine army, so it was no surprise that the English army was eventually heavily defeated. Despite this the northern earls had caused significant losses to the Norwegians, but their forces were so damaged that they were unable to play any further part in the campaigns of that year. It is this, rather than lack of support for King Harold, that undoubtedly best explains their absence at Hastings in October. Following the battle of Gate Fulford, the victorious Norwegians entered York.

While Edwin and Morcar were preparing their forces in the north and losing the battle, King Harold was issuing his third military summons of the year and he hastened north to assist his beleaguered noblemen. A mere five days after the defeat of the northern earls, Harold advanced through York to meet Harald Hardrada and Tostig at Stamford Bridge. They were taken completely by surprise by Harold's arrival. Before the battle began, Harold offered Tostig his earldom back if he would change sides, but Tostig threw the offer back in the king's face. Henry of Huntingdon also tells us that King Harold offered Harald Hardrada 'Six feet of ground or as much more as he needs, as he is taller than most men.'[8] It was fighting talk!

The Norwegians held a strong position, defending the bridge on the north-eastern bank of the River Derwent. Legend has it that a lone Viking axeman held the bridge against all comers for hours, until a sneaky Englishman paddled under the bridge in a barrel and thrust a spear up through the wooden slats. The crescendo of the battle came with the deaths of both Harald Hardrada and Tostig. With this, the morale of the Norwegians was broken and they began to flee. This retreat quickly became a rout and only twenty-four ships were required to carry the survivors home – from the original force of 300 ships.

Harold had won the day, but at a price. His army was tired and badly mauled, and he had lost the forces of both the Earl of Northumbria and the Earl of Mercia for any further combat that year. However, he had proved himself a decisive and effective military leader and doubtless must have thought his throne was now secure. Had he won at Hastings we would probably now recall him as 'King Harold the Great!' His victory at Stamford Bridge had crushed the Viking threat and seemed to signal the end of the Viking Wars.

Autumn 1066: the Norman invasion

However, Stanford Bridge did *not* mark the end of the Viking Wars: it was at this point that William decided to make his move. Having sailed his fleet to St Valéry sur Somme, he waited for the wind to be in the right direction. The same winds that had brought Harald Hardrada to England had turned and the conditions were right for William to begin his invasion.

On 27 September, just two days after the Battle of Stamford Bridge, William set sail, crossing the channel overnight and landing in Pevensey in Sussex. Once ashore, William ordered that some of his boats be symbolically burnt, while the rest were dismantled and pulled ashore. Later sources tell of how William slipped as he stepped ashore, leading to dismay amongst his men who saw this as a bad omen; however, William was quick to retort as he stooped on the beach with his hands full of sand, 'See, my lords, by the splendour of God, I have taken possession of England with both my hands. It is now mine, and what is mine is yours.'[9]

An earth embankment was built across the harbour mouth to protect the ships from the weather and a castle was constructed at the top of the hill. The Normans then proceeded to pillage and burn the surrounding area: William had landed in the heart of Godwin territory and doubtless knew that Harold would come rushing south to the aid of his own people. However, William did not move very far from his original landing point and it is unclear exactly what his rationale was for doing this, given that he could hardly have expected to conquer a kingdom without venturing further into it. It seems likely, in the wake of Harold's decisive victory at Stamford Bridge, that he felt the greatest likelihood of success lay in him maintaining a defensive position and making Harold come to him. It worked.

Harold did not hesitate and, upon hearing of William's landing, he raced his army south as quickly as they had been marched north, stopping only at his foundation of Waltham Abbey to pray for victory. By around 12 October he was back in London with the remains of his troops from the northern campaign, and gathering reinforcements. Once these reinforcements had arrived, Harold began the 60-mile (100km) trek to Sussex. Harold ordered his men to meet at the 'hoary apple tree', a local Sussex landmark. The stage was set for one of the most important battles in English history.

Saturday, 14 October 1066: the Battle of Hastings

While Harold's exhausted men rested at the 'hoary apple tree', William's troops kept watch throughout the night and when dawn broke advanced on the English army. Despite being taken by surprise, Harold assembled his troops and moved them into position on Senlac Ridge, about a mile from their overnight camp – this was the best defensive position in the area. Harold's army would have been made up of two elements: *huscarls*, who were elite members of his personal retinue, and the fyrd, made up of less well-trained and disciplined reservists. Harold would have tried to intersperse the two to maintain discipline and order. However, it appears from the later events of the battle that he may not have had time to fully complete this.

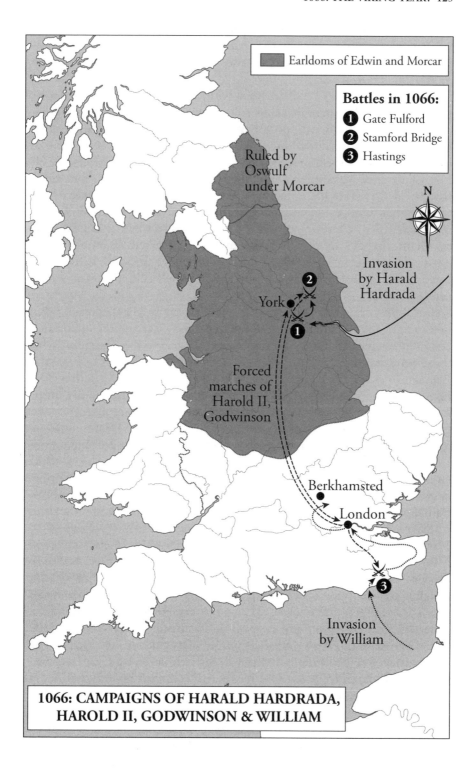

Earldoms of Edwin and Morcar

Battles in 1066:
1. Gate Fulford
2. Stamford Bridge
3. Hastings

N

Ruled by
Oswulf
under Morcar

Invasion
by Harald
Hardrada

York

Forced
marches of
Harold II,
Godwinson

Berkhamsted

London

Invasion
by William

**1066: CAMPAIGNS OF HARALD HARDRADA,
HAROLD II, GODWINSON & WILLIAM**

The Normans were at a disadvantage. Despite having taken Harold by surprise they were having to attack uphill and, as a result, the Norman knights found it much harder to be effective in their impact on the Anglo-Saxon line. Harold's best option was to fight a defensive battle and to rely on the much-vaunted English shield-wall, behind which his men could stand while the Norman attacks broke themselves on it.

The defensive tactic was initially a great success. Time and time again, the Norman knights hurled themselves against the English shields but, as the Bayeux Tapestry shows, they were unable to make any headway. The English defence was taking its toll on the Norman troops and the Breton troops on the left wing collapsed, leading to widespread panic among the Norman troops including the spreading of a rumour that William had been killed. As the Normans fell back, a section of the English army began to advance in pursuit of what they perceived to be a defeated enemy. However, once down from their defensive position at the top of the hill the English troops were surrounded by William's army and cut off.

Both armies had been equally mauled and now re-grouped and continued to fight into the afternoon. In an attempt to recreate the breaking of the English line, William ordered a series of feigned retreats, but while these resulted in a number of casualties it was not enough to break the English shield wall. As the afternoon wore on and the English stood firm, it looked increasingly likely that they would be the victors on the field. If they could hold on until nightfall (about 6pm in mid-October), then reinforcements would arrive the next day; but William could not make up his losses overnight. Things were critical for the Normans as the shadows lengthened. In a desperate last attempt, William threw all his troops – archers, infantry and cavalry – forward in a final push. Norman arrows rained down on the enemy on top of the hill. As a result of this, there appears to have been a weakening of the English line and the death of King Harold.

It is unclear exactly how Harold died. Traditionally, of course, he was killed by an arrow in the eye. The *Carmen*, written by Guy, Bishop of Amiens, shortly after the battle, says that Harold was killed by four knights and his body was brutally dismembered. Amatus of Montecassino's *L'Ystoire de li Normant* (*History of the Normans*), written thirty years after the Battle of Hastings, is the first report of Harold being shot in the eye with an arrow. The Bayeux Tapestry gives a confused picture of the death of Harold. A figure in the panel of the Bayeux Tapestry with the inscription '*Harold Rex Interfectus Est*' (Harold the King is killed) is depicted gripping an arrow that has struck his eye, but some historians have questioned whether this man is intended to be Harold, or if Harold is intended as the next figure lying to the right almost prone, being mutilated beneath a horse's hooves. It may be that both accounts are accurate:

that Harold suffered first the eye wound, then the mutilation, and that the Bayeux Tapestry is correct in depicting both, in sequence.

However Harold died, his death brought an end to the battle. Without their king, the English army was broken; the Anglo-Saxon cause was destroyed. It is likely that it was at this point in the battle that Harold's brothers Gyrth and Leofwine were also killed, leading to the Norman capture of the royal standard. As evening fell on the 14 October, England's last Anglo-Saxon king lay dead upon the battlefield surrounded by his brothers and his *huscarls*, and the remnants of his army were scattered. This was the death of Anglo-Saxon England.

The body of Harold was eventually recovered. However, he had been so badly mutilated that he could only be identified by Edith Swan-neck, Harold's long-term *more danico* wife; she was able to identify the body by marks known only to her. William apparently refused to give the body to Gytha, Harold's mother, for burial even when she offered its weight in gold and he, instead, ordered the body to be buried on the sea shore. Local tradition from Waltham Abbey records that Harold's body was eventually disinterred and laid to rest in Waltham, which had been founded by Harold. Later Augustinian canons (concerned at a 'Harold cult' developing) encouraged pre-existing legends that Harold had survived the battle and travelled to the continent seeking allies, and then later lived as a hermit in Chester or Canterbury (the former tradition recorded by the Norman-Welsh cleric, Gerald of Wales, in the 1190s). This tradition may reflect the fact that Harold's posthumous son – Harold Haroldson, by Queen Edith – was born in Chester, where she had taken refuge on her way out of the country.

Tradition has it that William gave thanks to God for his victory and ordered that all in his army should do penance for the souls that they had killed that day. He himself paid for the foundation of Battle Abbey, with its High Altar located on the spot where Harold fell.

What happened next?

Harold may have been dead and the battle may have been over, but the contest for England was only just beginning. William kept his army in Hastings for about a week, then he marched through south-eastern England, via Dover and Canterbury, to London Bridge.

Finding this too heavily defended, he continued along the southern bank of the Thames to Wallingford, sending a detachment to take Winchester on the way. By now it was December, and the long year of waiting and fighting had exhausted the English will to resist. Dover and Southwark had been razed to the ground, and William now had control of Canterbury, the religious centre of England, and Winchester, the ceremonial seat of the ancient Anglo-Saxon and more recent Anglo-Danish kings. Importantly, control of Winchester also meant control of the royal treasury.

At Wallingford, the first English submissions occurred. Archbishop Stigand of Canterbury led a delegation of important English bishops and thegns, who surrendered to William, and the gates of Wallingford were opened to him. The English delegation included the rightful heir to the throne, Edgar Ætheling. By Christmas, the earls Edwin, Morcar and Waltheof, along with Archbishop Ealdred of York, had also surrendered, having ensured that their positions would be secure under the new Norman regime.

After this, William was able to enter London freely and was crowned by Archbishop Ealdred on Christmas Day, in Westminster Abbey. Significantly, this was the same place in which Harold had been crowned almost a year earlier. Also, Westminister Abbey was Edward the Confessor's foundation and, by choosing to be crowned there, William may have been deliberately stressing the continuity between himself and the old Anglo-Saxon order. He also ensured that he was crowned by Ealdred and not Stigand, whose legitimacy, as we have seen earlier, was rejected by the pope.

During the ceremony, the assembled magnates (both Norman and English) shouted their acclamation of the new king. However, their shouts startled the guards outside the church who, fearing an uprising, promptly set fire to the neighbouring buildings. This was a destructive beginning to a new era of English history.

Why did William win at Hastings?

William was helped at Hastings by the failed Viking invasion of Harald Hardrada. When, in mid-October, Harold Godwinson attempted the same kind of rapid advance to battle that had earlier caught Harald Hardrada and his Viking army by surprise, he found the Normans far from being taken unawares. The march north, which cost the English both men and time, and then the long march south, had allowed the Normans a crucial breathing space, which they had used to secure their bridgehead. Anglo-Saxon casualties had been high at the battles of Gate Fulford and Stamford Bridge, and the northern earls were so mauled that they were unable to participate in the campaign against William. The later Norman poet, Wace, believed that the Anglo-Saxon forces had been significantly weakened by the campaign in the north. Similarly, John of Worcester also recorded the tradition that important English warriors had been lost at Gate Fulford and at Stamford Bridge.[10]

In reflecting on the stress on troops of the forced-marching north and then south in 1066 it has been calculated that the Anglo-Saxon fighting men carried at least 70lb (32kg) in weight in the form of mail, shield, sword, axe and helmet.[11] Without a doubt the failed intervention by Harald Hardrada had taken its toll of Harold and his army.

Despite this, Hastings was still a very hard-fought battle and victory only came to William after a long day of fighting. When Harold died, it was in the middle of his personal bodyguard of *huscarls*. This was the fighting force that had been inherited from Cnut. They died wielding that peculiarly Viking weapon, the two handed battle-axe.[12] There were, therefore, many echoes of the Viking Wars on that October hillside, as the light faded and the Norman arrows fell on Harold.

It seemed that the Viking impact on England was finally over. Harald Hardrada of Norway was dead; Svein Esthrithson of Denmark had not intervened; Harold the Anglo-Saxon had fallen; the Normans (descendants of Vikings) had won. It seemed to be over ... but it was not over. Not yet.

CHAPTER 10

The Vikings Return!

It might be thought that, with the defeat of Harold Godwinson at Hastings in October 1066, the impact of the Vikings on the Norman Conquest was over. What has been the theme of this book would appear to have been completed: the Vikings had been the biggest single cause of the events of 1066.

The end of an era?

The effects of Harald Hardrada's unsuccessful invasion had been one of the key factors leading to the defeat of the Anglo-Saxon army at Hastings. It was the final way in which Viking involvement had led to the historic events of 1066 and the Norman victory. The death of Harold Godwinson on Saturday 14 October 1066, may seem a fitting end to the Viking Wars that had impacted on English history since the first raid on Portland had occurred way back in 789.

In the autumn of 1066 the last great Viking invasion, which had threatened to repeat the success of Cnut in 1016, had been decisively crushed at the Battle of Stamford Bridge. On that single day the ambitions of Harald Hardrada of Norway had been cut down, along with Harald and most of his army. Then, at Hastings, the descendants of Viking colonists – albeit ones who had become assimilated to French culture – had succeeded in killing the last Anglo-Saxon king of England and a great many of the leading men of southern England, the Normans having landed in Sussex while Harold Godwinson was far away, facing the Viking invasion that had occurred in Yorkshire. The Battle of Hastings, therefore, can arguably be seen as the last great act in Scandinavian involvement in English affairs that had dominated society and politics since 789. It certainly appeared to have completed a process that had started with Cnut's Viking Conquest of 1016.

Over, but not over...

However, the matter was not yet over. Even after the events of the autumn of 1066 the Vikings of Scandinavia continued to exert an influence on English affairs. This is because what occurred at Hastings was, of course, only the beginning of the process that we now know as the

'Norman Conquest'. When William was crowned king on Christmas Day in 1066 nobody yet knew what kind of king he was going to be and what kind of regime he was going to establish. What happened at Hastings was only the 'victory'; what occurred over the next twenty years was the 'Conquest'. And it was these twenty years that were to change irrevocably the course of English and indeed British history.

England had experienced conquest before, of course, and the events of 1016 and its consequences were very apparent in the second half of the eleventh century. That event and its effects had been intimately interwoven with the politics of Scandinavia as we have seen so far. What is striking is that these factors continued to play an active role within English politics after 1066. In short, the Vikings had not finished with England and the ambitions of Scandinavian rulers would continue to influence the course of events in England in the generation after 1066, just as they had done so in the generation before that seismic event. Even after the Norman Conquest of 1066, the Vikings (in the form of kings of Denmark) continued to intervene in England and it was this intervention that significantly affected the way that the Norman Conquest developed and also led to the production of one of the key documents of the Norman Conquest: the *Domesday Book* of 1086.

In the twenty years that followed the Battle of Hastings the threat of further Viking intervention hung over William and the new Norman regime. It encouraged English resistance to the Normans and threatened William's rule. The Norman response to this threat would change the character of the new regime and would help define the nature of the Norman Conquest. In 1066 the Viking impact on eleventh-century England was far from over.[1]

Anglo-Saxon resistance to the Normans ... the Viking connection

Given the damage and chaos caused by earlier Viking raids and conquest, it might come as something of a surprise to discover that Scandinavian involvement was the single biggest factor leading to English resistance to the new Norman regime of William the Conqueror. But that is exactly what occurred.

Without a doubt there would always have been resistance. Despite the death of Harold and his brothers at Hastings and despite the absence of a credible warrior candidate capable of mounting an armed response to William's military machine, there would eventually have been rebellions. William needed to reward his followers and there were going to be many Anglo-Saxon 'losers' as the spoils of victory were passed around the Normans.

Even with the proviso that William could *perhaps* claim to be within his rights when he seized estates owned by the Godwinsons and others who had fallen at Hastings, this would still have left dispossessed and resentful heirs who would constitute the raw material from which resistance to Norman rule could be forged. And this action by William was very much open to question since, before he was consecrated as king on Christmas Day 1066, how could those resisting him be described as 'rebels'? It was victor's justice and implied that 'the English were in rebellion against the king even before he was consecrated and this forms the ideological basis for the dispossession of those who died in resisting the Norman invasion'.[2] Only those who survived and were therefore able to submit to William could keep their land; those who had died had their land forfeited to the king. This land seizure fell heavily on eastern Wessex, the east Midlands and East Anglia, for it was from these areas that the army that was defeated at Hastings was largely recruited.[3]

The matter was even more complex than this. Even in the early days of the Norman regime it became clear that legal niceties would not be standing in the way of the victors. William might promise to rule in the traditions of the earlier Anglo-Saxon kings (ignoring the usurper Harold Godwinson) and to be the legitimate successor to King Edward the Confessor, but in the countryside Norman lords soon began dispossessing Anglo-Saxon landowners. This was a process that would accelerate as we shall see (and Scandinavian intervention unwittingly played a part in that), but we can be sure that it was hard-wired into the Norman victory *from the start*.

There is plenty of evidence to support this view. English churchmen were replaced by Norman and French competitors at Winchcombe and Malmesbury; and the role of Bishop of Dorchester-on-Thames went to a monk from Fécamp within just three years of Hastings in this case. The strategic area of Sussex was soon dominated by knights who had accompanied William in 1066 and Kent looked like it would go the same way.[4] As early as 1067 the compiler of manuscript *E* of the *Anglo-Saxon Chronicle* complained that 'He [William] gave away every man's land when he came back [from Normandy].' The compiler of manuscript *D* adds the comment 'The king imposed a heavy tax on the wretched people, and nevertheless caused all that they overran to be ravaged.'[5] The later chronicler John of Worcester described the tax of 1068 as 'insupportable'. Life under the Normans was tough and things were about to get a whole lot worse. And in this process Scandinavian influence would play a decisive role.

In 1068, a revolt at Exeter against Norman rule ended in failure. After this revolt collapsed, Harold Godwinson's mother, Gytha, who had been heavily involved in the resistance, shifted her base of anti-Norman operations to the island of Flatholme in the Bristol Channel. In so doing, she imitated the traditional activities of Scandinavian fleets in this area: the island had earlier been used as a base by Viking raiders since the ninth century. After failing to raise the West Country in a successful revolt, those who had been defeated reacted by raiding their own country, which was now under Norman rule.

These members of the defeated English nobility were adopting the very Viking tactics that had earlier troubled England. They were, in effect, morphing into 'Vikings' and would soon find they had more in common with Scandinavian rulers than with the new rulers of their own country. This is clear in the way that Harold Godwinson's grown-up sons (by his first marriage to Edith Swan-neck) sought assistance from King Diarmait of Dublin and returned to England, later in 1068, accompanied by a force of Irish-Norse mercenaries in fifty-two ships. They were now operating in the tradition of earlier Viking raiders who had used Irish ports from which to sail against England. Those who observed these actions at the time unconsciously noted the similarity.

In manuscript *E* of the *Anglo-Saxon Chronicle* the word *lið* ('seaborne military') is used to describe both the forces of Harold Godwinson's exiled sons who were operating out of Dublin and those of Svein Estrithson of Denmark, who invaded England in 1069–70.[6] The word *lið* is a hybrid one arising from Old English and Old Norse, and was used to describe Viking ship-crews. For example, a poem survives called *Liðsmannaflokkr*, which describes an attack on London. A poem known as a *flokkr* was one without a refrain, so this title basically means 'Poem of the men of the fleet'; the fleet in question was Cnut's fleet that conquered England in 1016. The poem purports to date from Cnut's period and perhaps to have been composed by members of his household army, although any attribution and date of composition is uncertain. What matters, in the context of the later 1060s, is that the word described a Viking fleet and yet by the late 1060s it could be used to describe one of these *and* a fleet operated by exiled Anglo-Saxon ex-nobles. The years of rule by Cnut, Harald Harefoot and Harthacnut – coupled with the aftermath of 1066 – had interwoven England and Scandinavia so as to produce a situation whereby it was hard to tell the difference between Vikings and some Anglo-Saxons.

The first attack by Harold Godwinson's sons was on Bristol, where 'the citizens fought against them fiercely'.[7] This is rather a surprise: after all, it was only a year since Exeter had risen against Norman rule under the leadership of their mother, so why did Bristol fail to support them? The answer is that at Bristol they were seen as Viking-style raiders and not as liberators from Norman rule. The way that the disappointed sons of Harold then behaved in the face of this disappointment rather justified the decision by the people of Bristol: they raided the coastal settlements of Somerset. In this they were showing the *modus operandi* traditionally associated with Viking raiders. They succeeded in defeating a local English force and killing its commander, who was named Eadnoth the

Staller; he had earlier served their father but had now transferred his allegiance to the Normans. Following this attack on fellow countrymen, Harold's sons finally returned to Ireland. But they had not given up.

In 1069, this fleet of Anglo-Irish-Norse adventurers returned, and again raided the south-west of England. However, they were no more successful than in their previous attempt, and by the end of the year they had been defeated by the Normans, who then went on to establish strongholds in the West Country to prevent further trouble.[8] What is interesting is the fact that there was no popular support for these Anglo-Norse invaders. They were simply regarded as pirates.[9] As such, they were resisted by both Normans and Anglo-Saxons. After failing to rally support in Somerset, their base on the island of Flatholme was abandoned.

What happened next only further emphasized how closely entwined were the politics of England and Scandinavia. While the women found refuge with a relative by marriage, the Count of Flanders (a popular bolt-hole for the Godwin clan), the surviving sons of Harold Godwinson went to Denmark, to the court of King Svein Estrithson. A lot had changed since 1016, for now they could view this as friendly territory. The changes in Anglo-Scandinavian connections since 1016 meant that a situation now existed in which a Danish king – Svein Estrithson – was cousin to a dead Anglo-Saxon king, Harold Godwinson. And, as we saw in Chapter 8, in the 1040s it was Godwin of Wessex (Harold's father and an Anglo-Dane) who had urged Edward the Confessor to assist Svein Estrithson in his struggle for independence from Magnus the Good, King of Norway.[10] There was, therefore, a close connection between Godwin's family and the King of Denmark – yet another of the consequences that flowed from Cnut's Viking Conquest. Disappointingly, we do not know how Svein Estrithson responded to the request for Danish aid against the Normans from these exiled sons of Harold Godwinson. They then vanish from history after Svein died in 1074.

What we *do know* is that Svein Estrithson had a track record of intervening in England on the back of his relationships with the Anglo-Danish rulers of England and some at least of their Anglo-Danish elites. In the 1040s he clearly believed that he was a contender for the English throne and may even have been planning an invasion to support this claim in 1047.[11] He revived this claim after 1066 and his revival of the Viking connection was to have a profound effect on the way in which the Norman Conquest developed.

An indecisive Viking king: the disastrous interventions of Svein Estrithson after 1066

Prior to the arrival of the sons of Harold Godwinson, Svein Estrithson had already intervened in England in an attempt to secure the English throne for himself. With Harold Godwinson and Harald Hardrada of Norway both dead, the way seemed open to revive the Danish claim on the crown of England. Svein clearly did not feel that the Norman victory should prevent him from so doing even though, in 1066, he had provided some diplomatic support for the Norman invasion. The Norman success had not taken the edge off of his own ambitions;[12] ambitions that had been on hold since the mid-1040s.

The question was: how best to pursue these ambitions in the changed world of the 1060s and the 1070s? Svein Estrithson's first strategy was to provide assistance to English anti-Norman rebels such as Waltheof, Earl of Huntingdon and his northern allies, Edgar Ætheling, and Hereward the Wake in the Fens of East Anglia. All of these resisted Norman rule with one eye looking to Scandinavia for assistance. This hope seemed justified since, in 1069, Svein Estrithson invaded northern England. Only three years earlier another Viking king – Harald Hardrada of Norway – had followed the same route and had been successfully resisted. But times had changed since the autumn of 1066, and by 1069 a Scandinavian intervention seemed far preferable to the Norman rule of William. Exactly how all these competing ambitions were to be reconciled once Norman rule was overthrown is a little difficult to imagine! Both Edgar Ætheling and Svein Estrithson, for example, both thought the crown was theirs by right.

Early in 1069, Edgar Ætheling returned from exile in Scotland because a major revolt had broken out against Norman rule in northern England. When that revolt was crushed by William, Edgar retreated again to Scotland. It seemed as if the Norman knights had successfully seen off the threat. However, late in the campaigning season, Svein Estrithson launched a new Viking bid for the English throne. His fleet was later said to have numbered 240 ships and it was commanded by Svein Estrithson's son (and name-sake of an earlier mighty Viking king), Cnut (later Cnut IV of Denmark, also known as Cnut the Holy).

The fleet sailed down the North Sea and into the English Channel where it appeared off Dover, before sailing north along the Kentish coast and finally landing at Sandwich, Ipswich and finally near Norwich. Clearly, they were hoping that their arrival would provoke an English revolt. However, in none of these places was there sufficient English support for a major uprising. This is not surprising since Kent had suffered from Norman violence following the Battle of Hastings and people there knew how Normans treated resistance. There might have been more chance in East Anglia but there, too, people were cowed by Norman might. We cannot be exactly sure of when the great Norman castle was constructed at Norwich but it was certainly there by 1075 when it was the centre of a revolt led by Ralph de Gael, Earl of East Anglia, against William: the so-called 'Revolt of the Earls' (*see* below). The castle of 1075 was probably a large ring-work, and its construction may well have occurred by

1069, as part of the Norman attempt to control this important region of England. East Anglia, as well as being strategically important (Svein Forkbeard had seized Norwich in 1004 and Svein Estrithson attempted the same in 1069), was also economically highly significant as a food-producing area, and was one of the most highly populated medieval regions of England. In 1069, Svein Estrithson failed to take control of it and this was probably due to the Norman presence in the region.

The Danish fleet finally arrived in the Humber estuary, as so many other Viking fleets had done in the past. Having finally established a bridgehead, the Danish army was soon joined by Edgar Ætheling from Scotland and by Waltheof, the Anglo-Saxon Earl of Huntingdon. This curious alliance of the Viking king of Denmark, the rightful heir to the throne of England, an Anglo-Saxon earl and the northern English then crushed the Norman forces at York. Following this they seized control of Northumbria. The Anglo-Danish army refused to be drawn into a decisive battle with the Normans, and William was distracted by an English revolt that had broken out in the Midlands.[13] This stand-off meant that things hung in the balance in the early autumn of 1069; it was not to remain this way. Once William had suppressed the revolt in the Midlands, in November 1069, he turned his attention to the north.

Had Svein Estrithson and Edgar Ætheling succeeded in defeating William it is possible that they envisaged a division of the kingdom such as that which had occurred between Cnut and Edmund Ironside in 1016. If so, the history of England would have followed a different trajectory. But it was not to be, for William responded with devastating force, retaking York in December 1069, and driving his opponents to the Humber estuary. It was then that William began the ruthless destruction of opposition that today is remembered as the 'Harrying of the North'. This occurred through the winter of 1069–70. As well as crushing English opposition and terrorising the survivors so that no further revolts would occur, it is also likely that William intended to make the area unattractive to the Danish crown.[14] With its population and economy devastated, kings of Denmark might think twice about making a play for the area in the future. Viking intervention was helping to define the Norman Conquest. Without meaning to, it had inadvertently helped lead to the Harrying of the North.

Despite this devastation, Svein Estrithson still joined his son in the Humber estuary in the spring of 1070. Clearly, he had not yet given up on his English ambitions. In June 1070 a section of the Danish fleet sailed down the east coast to give assistance to yet another English rebel. This was Hereward, later called 'the Wake' (the 'watchful'). They sacked Peterborough (Cambridgeshire).[15] This was another one of those actions (like the attack on Bristol) in which the financing of military adventures was based on loot seized from unfortunate civilians – again, all very 'Viking'. In this case, though, they may have argued that they were deny-ing financial resources to the new Norman abbot of Peterborough.

Hereward himself was a landowner in Lincolnshire and was probably from an Anglo-Danish family,[16] just as Godwin had been in Sussex. The Viking Wars had created ethnic complexity across East Anglia, whereby a landowner of Danish ancestry could pose as an 'Anglo-Saxon' resist-ance hero. Hereward first appeared in 1070, plundering the abbey at Peterborough with the kind of 'justification' that we have just exam-ined. Manuscript E of the *Chronicle* states that part of Svein Estrithson's army arrived in nearby Ely and that the local English rose up in support of them. Manuscript E was compiled at Peterborough in the 1120s to replace a lost original, and was well informed with regard to East Anglian events. The easy way in which this alliance of Anglo-Danes from East Anglia and Danish warriors of Svein Estrithson operated reminds us of just how far East Anglia had become Anglo-Danish by the eleventh century.[17]

News soon reached Peterborough Abbey that its own tenants were planning to plunder the abbey because they had heard that it was to be given to a Norman; the looting of religious houses should not just be seen as a Viking activity. If it had become associated with an unpopular abbot then it was fair game to its own tenants. The *Chronicle* describes 'Hereward and his following' (who were accompanied by members of the Danish army) as 'outlaws'.[18] Clearly, the later compilers of this manu-script of the *Chronicle* found it difficult to decide who was friend and who was foe as they looked back on these events. Following the attack, the *Chronicle* records that the Anglo-Saxon bishop, Æthelric, excommu-nicated those responsible. Later Peterborough monastic tradition adapted the story to present Hereward as seizing the monastic treasure in order to prevent it falling into Norman hands.[19] This was clearly a patriotic attempt to salvage something positive out of a very difficult episode.

It was then that the wavering commitment of Svein Estrithson to his English ambitions was revealed. As the Normans counter-attacked and the English resistance faded, he was bought-off by the Normans. This was typical of Viking interventions in the past but it left his English allies dangerously exposed when the Danes left Ely with their loot. At the same time revolts elsewhere in England were also failing. But as long as Ely held out there was a safe haven for leaders of these failed revolts. These included Morcar, who had been the Earl of Northumbria, until replaced by William after 1066, along with several hundred supporters. The 'safe haven' would not survive for long. By the end of 1071, the revolt at Ely had collapsed. The Normans had attacked it by sea and by land across a causeway-bridge. The latter had helped them reach the rebels' base on the island of Ely. All the remaining rebels surrendered, with the exception of

Hereward and his immediate supporters. These continued to resist from the marshes and they vanish from any reliable historical account and move into legend.

This brings us back to the Scandinavian connection. The limited written records of Hereward's failed revolt show that it was heavily dependent on Danish support. The *Chronicle* records the start of the revolt after the initial Danish intervention in 1069; once that support was withdrawn, the revolt quickly collapsed. Only Scandinavian assistance could turn these local revolts into real challenges to Norman power, and this assistance was denied to Hereward as 1070 progressed. Svein Estrithson's intervention had once again encouraged English resistance, failed to follow through and had brought down a devastating Norman response. It was as a result of such revolts that William gave up his attempts to learn English and embarked on wholesale land seizure. Some of the most vicious aspects of the Norman Conquest can be tied to the unforeseen effects of – ineffective – Scandinavian interventions.

There was one other footnote in history that occurred because of the failure of the great northern revolt of 1069–70 and that, curiously, again linked the family of Harold Godwinson with the Viking north of Europe. As the northern uprisings faltered, Edith, the second wife of Harold Godwinson and sister of earls Edwin and Morcar, fled with her infant son by him (born after Harold's death) to Dublin. This son, Harold Haroldson, was then taken on to Norway where he was well received by Harald Hardrada's son, King Magnus II Haraldsson (King of Norway from 1066 to 1069). According to the twelfth-century historian, William of Malmesbury, this was because Harold Godwinson had shown mercy to the Viking survivors of the Battle of Stamford Bridge in the autumn of 1066.[20] Harold Haroldson is last heard of in 1098, fighting against a Norman army in North Wales as a member of a Viking fleet led by the new king of Norway, Magnus III Barelegs (ruler of Norway from 1093 until 1103 and ruler of the Kingdom of Man and the Isles from 1099 until 1103). He had become a Viking, but from that point he vanishes from history.

But to return to 1070: the collapse of the two great revolts would have far-reaching consequences. Edgar Ætheling was forced to flee once more to Scotland. Following yet another unsuccessful anti-Norman expedition in 1074, Edgar was finally reconciled to William: he would take part in no further revolts and died in 1125. William's magnanimity in accepting Edgar's submission may be explained by the fact that William no longer felt threatened by revolts in England. What is surprising, perhaps, is that despite these catastrophic failures, Viking rulers continued to intervene in English politics in the 1070s and 1080s.

In 1075, Svein Estrithson's son, Cnut IV of Denmark (Cnut the Holy), again returned to England. This time, though, he came with a mixed

Danish and Norwegian fleet of 'two hundred ships'.[21] This adventure was prompted by two main factors. First, in Denmark, Svein Estrithson had died in 1074[22] and this had led to a disputed succession between his sons Cnut and Harald. Harald eventually won, becoming King Harald III, and drove Cnut into exile in Sweden. Cnut then allied himself with Olaf III ('the Peaceful') of Norway. Cnut clearly hoped that, with Norwegian help, he might take the English throne. No doubt Olaf III thought that the assistance given to Cnut by Norway would ensure future support for Norway in any conflicts with Denmark.

The second factor was provided by an alliance between the one surviving Anglo-Saxon earl and two disaffected Norman earls. This is today remembered as the 'Revolt of the Earls'. It involved two Norman nobles – Ralph de Gael, Earl of East Anglia, and Roger de Breteuil, Earl of Hereford – in alliance with the Anglo-Saxon earl, Waltheof, Earl of Northumbria. Waltheof had earlier, in 1069, taken part in the failed northern revolt of Edgar Ætheling in alliance with Svein Estrithson of Denmark. When that revolt had failed he had made his peace with William, been restored to his earldom and gone on to marry William's niece, Judith. In 1072, he was appointed Earl of Northumbria in addition to his earldom of Huntingdon. But in 1075 he was once again (unwisely and disastrously) drawn into yet another rebellion; one that, as in 1069, was dependent on Scandinavian support. Ralph de Gael sailed to Scandinavia to solicit help, his reward being the mixed fleet referred to earlier. The assistance, though, was ineffective. A pattern is emerging here: by the time the Danish-Norwegian fleet arrived, the 'Revolt of the Earls' had ended. The response of the Scandinavians was predictable. Cnut landed in the Humber estuary and sacked York. It was a repeat of the failed invasion of 1069–70: an adventure that had started as a great political intervention had, once more, ended as a Viking plundering raid. It could have been 1015.

With the revolt crushed by decisive Norman action, Ralph and Roger lost their lands (Roger was also imprisoned, but released on William's death in 1087), but Waltheof was beheaded. Cnut, on the other hand, later retrieved his position in Denmark on the death of his brother, Harald III, in 1080. Cnut (now ruling as Cnut IV, later called 'the Holy') then ruled Denmark until his death in 1086. However, he had not given up on his English ambitions: in his last great intervention, he would help give rise to one of the most famous and enduring monuments to the Norman Conquest.

The ambitions of Cnut IV of Denmark and the Domesday survey, 1085–6

Domesday Book, a land survey commissioned by William the Conqueror and carried out in 1086, is one of the great monuments to the Norman Conquest. Along with Norman castles, it symbolises the transformation brought by the aftermath of 1066 and the power and ambitions of the Normans. Its aim was to establish land ownership in England and the extent of the taxes that could be raised from this land. William commissioned the survey while meeting with his leading nobles at Gloucester during Christmas, 1085.

As well as establishing taxation values, the *Domesday Book* also records which manors belonged to which estates. It identifies the King's barons: the tenants-in-chief who held land directly from the king and who owed him military service in the form of knights to fight in his campaigns. The king clearly wanted to ensure that nobody paid less than was owed (in terms of tax or knight-service). The survey also established just what had happened to land ownership as a result of the huge dispossessions that had taken place due to the Norman Conquest. It settled disputes and established property titles. In this way it completed the process of change that had started in 1066 and recorded the results. There is today some debate over whether William the Conqueror actually intended the results to be written up into a book or whether this was due to a decision made during the reign of his successor, William II 'Rufus'.

Royal commissioners were sent out around England to collect and record the information required. England was divided into seven regions, or 'circuits', and three or four commissioners were assigned to each circuit. The tenants-in-chief and sheriffs (local royal officials) drew up lists of all manors and land holders in each county. These returns were compared with existing tax records, drawing on the Anglo-Saxon legacy of centralized record keeping and local county courts. Much of this system had developed, ironically, as a way by which the challenges posed by the Viking Wars could be met; and now it was being used to chart the consequences of a series of events that had themselves occurred as an outworking of those very same wars. A reassessment of the tax burden (the *geld*) also took place at about the same time as the Domesday survey occurred and still survives for the south-west. This gives more detail than survives in the final record of *Domesday Book* itself.

The commissioners visited each county court and checked the accuracy of the information they had received by calling juries from the local areas (the hundreds), who swore oaths as to the accuracy of the information being assessed. It was then that disputes were settled with, no doubt, pressure brought to bear by newly established Norman lords to ensure that disputes were settled in their favour (there is evidence of this). The information collected recorded the value of the estates as it was in the time of King Edward the Confessor, what it was when William gave it, and its value in 1086. It was also to be noted whether more taxes could be collected from the estate than were being taken in 1086.

When all the information had been checked and gathered it was edited, arranged into counties, then sorted, but not by place. Instead, the information was listed according to the social hierarchy of the owner. This started with the king and then ran downwards through the great landowners, starting with the great Church landowners. Under each of these landowners the land was described by each local area (the so-called hundreds or *wapentakes*) and then listed by the manor (the local estate itself). It was then written down in Latin in regional returns or 'circuit summaries' as the first stage in the process of writing up the results.

Today, *Domesday Book* survives as two volumes. Each of these represents a different stage in the process of how *Domesday* was originally compiled. The smaller of the volumes is called *Little Domesday* and is an example of an earlier stage in the writing up process (the 'circuit summary' stage). It covers the counties of Essex, Norfolk and Suffolk. The information from *Little Domesday* was never entered into *Great Domesday* and, as a consequence, *Little Domesday* was kept as the final record for East Anglia. The larger book, *Great Domesday*, represents the final stage in the production. It covers the areas of the country not covered in *Little Domesday*, with the exceptions of London, Winchester, Bristol and Tamworth. Its coverage of the north-west of England is limited; the counties of Durham and Northumberland are omitted; the coverage of Cumberland, Westmorland and north Lancashire is also limited to lands of the king and just two other tenants-in-chief. Coverage of south Lancashire is also limited. It does, though, include some border areas of Wales. *Great Domesday* has since been rebound in two parts and *Little Domesday* in three parts. It was called '*Domesday*' by the year 1180, as a reference to the Last Judgement Day and indicates that there was no appeal against its decisions. Before that date it was variously known as the *Winchester Roll* or the *King's Roll* or the *Book of the Treasury*.

As we have seen, there is a double connection between the compilation of *Domesday Book* and the Vikings. It used a tax system that was largely organized to meet the requirements of the Viking Wars and its com-pilation was ordered by a ruler (a descendant of Vikings) who had only achieved his success due to a range of factors set in play by the Viking Wars. However, the connection is more immediate even than these factors. For the decision to carry out the Domesday survey in 1085 was triggered by yet another Scandinavian intervention in English politics.

In 1080, Cnut finally succeeded his brother, Harald III, as King of Denmark (as Cnut IV). Five years later, in 1085, he began preparations for yet another invasion of England. In this he continued a tradition in Danish royal ambitions that dated back to Svein Forkbeard and the earlier Cnut at the beginning of the eleventh century. Cnut IV was the grand-nephew of the Cnut who had ruled England, Denmark and Norway until his death in 1035. As a result of that Viking Conquest, which had been added to by the complexities and promises that accompanied the reigns of Cnut's immediate successors in the second half of the 1030s and in the 1040s, Cnut IV believed that he had a strong claim to the English throne. It was a result of the same tangle of North Sea politics that had inspired similar ambitions in Svein Estrithson and in Harald Hardrada.

Cnut IV was supported once again by his ally Olaf III of Norway and also by his father-in-law, Count Robert I of Flanders. Although Robert I's sister (Matilda) was married to William the Conqueror, Flanders had earlier been a refuge for the Godwins (most recently the exiled Godwin women in 1069) and – in the shifting politics of the mid-1080s – Count Robert I threw his support behind his son-in-law, Cnut IV, and against his brother-in-law, William the Conqueror.

This time, though, the strength of the Norman defences seriously deterred the Danish elites. Their support was crucial to the success of the invasion and their reluctance severely weakened the enterprise. In addition, Cnut was also preoccupied because he felt threatened by Henry IV, the Holy Roman Emperor. There were tensions between the empire and both Denmark and Flanders because, in the case of the former, political exiles from the empire were being sheltered in Denmark. As Cnut hesitated, his army became unsettled as the time for the harvest approached and Cnut's brother became the spokesman for those who wished to stand down the army. As a result, there was no invasion in 1085 and Cnut made plans for it to occur in 1086. However, facing a renewed and more serious revolt, Cnut fled from the rebels and was assassinated in July 1086. The last great Viking threat had passed.[23] Cnut IV had planned to repeat the achievements of Svein Forkbeard and an earlier Cnut but his plans had come to nothing. Nevertheless, they had caused William, as a response to this threat of Danish invasion, to commission the Domesday survey in 1085.

According to the Anglo-Norman historian Orderic Vitalis, writing between 1114 and 1141, the survey aimed at clarifying the knight-service owed to the crown, 'ready to be mustered at a moment's notice in the king's service whenever necessary'.[24] This clarification was pressing because, as Orderic reminded his readers, 'Cnut the younger, king of Denmark was then preparing a great fleet, and making arrangements to invade England, conquered in earlier times by his ancestors Swein [Svein Forkbeard] and Cnut and claim his right.'[25] The impending threat of this invasion caused the survey to be set in motion.[26] Faced with the threat of Danish invasion in 1085, weaknesses in the national systems of taxation and defence needed fixing, fast. Tax and military obligations needed rapid clarification.[27] The result was the Domesday survey, which was eventually written up as the *Domesday Book*.

It is clear that Domesday had other purposes too, including sorting out the confused state of land titles caused by the upheaval and dispossessions following Norman victory. However, the trigger for its compilation was clearly the perceived threat that was posed by Cnut IV of Denmark in 1085. As King William prepared to celebrate Christmas at Gloucester that year, he had Vikings on his mind; one of the most striking legacies of the Norman Conquest was caused by a threat of Viking invasion.

CHAPTER 11

Pulling the Threads Together

The famous Icelandic poet, Sigvatr Thórðarson, was court poet to a number of Scandinavian rulers. These included Olaf II of Norway (ruled 1015–28), as well as Cnut of Denmark and England (ruled England 1016–35), Magnus Olafsson the Good, King of Norway (1035–47) and also Denmark (1042–7) and Anund Jacob, king of Sweden (ruled 1022–c.1050). Sigvatr wrote what is called 'skaldic' poetry, a particular kind of verse composed in Old Norse from the early ninth to the late fourteenth century. Its distinctive character lies in its complex structure and syntax, and metaphors known as *kennings*. It is deliberately obscure, using word-play, irony and ambiguity.[1] Sigvatr Thórðarson was a skald (an exponent of this type of poetry) and a Christian; about 160 verses of his poetry have survived. This is more than for any other poet from this period of time, since much Icelandic poetry (and that of Scandinavia generally) dates from much later than the events it describes or celebrates. Sigvatr claimed to have visited Rouen in Normandy in the 1020s. In his poem *Vestrfararvísur* (*Verses of Western Travel*) he wrote 'On many mornings do we remember how I made fast [my ship] in the west bay of Rouen.'[2] It is a reminder of how Normandy, England and the Viking world were so closely related in the eleventh century.

Sigvatr also wrote a skaldic poem called *Víkingavísur* (*Tune/Song about Vikings*), which charts the adventures of Olaf II Haraldsson (King of Norway 1015–28 and later sainted) as a young Viking, particularly his participation in the raids on England in the opening decades of the eleventh century. It also records how he campaigned in Brittany, Frisia, western France and Spain. Sigvatr also composed a memorial poem about Cnut of England, called the *Tøgdrápa* or *Knútsdrápa* (*Drápa* – a long series of poetic stanzas – *about Cnut*). Sadly, nothing remains of the verses he wrote for Svein Forkbeard of Denmark.

The view from Scandinavia

These poems give us a taste of the great events of the latest stages of the Viking Wars, but served up to a Scandinavian audience and geared to their poetic traditions. In a similar way we learn about some details of the events of 1066 only from Scandinavian sources. This reminds us that we must not only look at 1066 through an English or a Norman lens. There was a very strong Scandinavian take on the events, too; a Viking perspective on what led to 1066 and on the consequences of this momentous upheaval. *Morkinskinna* (intriguingly called *Mouldy parchment* due to the state of its surviving manuscript) is a saga relating the history of the Norwegian kings from c.1025 to 1157. It was written in Iceland in about 1220 and survives in a manuscript that dates from around 1275 (the so-called '*Mouldy parchment*'). *Morkinskinna* claims:

> And some men say that earl Tostig [Godwinson] sent Guthormr Gunnhildarson to meet with King Haraldr [Harald Hardrada] to offer him Northumbria with sworn oaths, and urge him to campaign in the west. And so Guthormr went to Norway.

Other Norse accounts preserve other traditions (some contradictory) concerning 1066, such as claiming that Tostig first approached Svein Estrithson of Denmark before turning to Harald Hardrada. This claim is found in *Fagrskinna* (in contrast to *Morkinskinna*, this manuscript's name means *Pretty parchment*). Or that he personally travelled to Norway to ask for help against his brother Harold – this is found in *Ágrip af Nóregskonungasögum* (*Compendium of the Sagas of the Kings of Norway*, a title coined for it in 1835), a history of the kings of Norway, composed in about 1190.

It is even claimed that Tostig travelled to Normandy 'to meet with his relatives'(?), while his ambassador travelled to Norway with his request for assistance from there. This statement is found in *Morkinskinna*, in a passage that contradicts other information about Tostig's movements found in this same account. The only non-Scandinavian writer who also claims that this trip to Normandy occurred is the Anglo-Norman chronicler, Orderic Vitalis, writing between 1114 and 1141.[3]

The events of 1066 are also referred to in a curious incident retold in the Icelandic manuscript *Flateyjarbók* (*Flat-island Book*, so named from an island in the Breiðafjörður fjord on the north-west coast of Iceland). This book constitutes the longest surviving Icelandic manuscript and contains mostly sagas of the Viking kings of Norway, along with sagas recording traditions about Norse colonization of Greenland, Orkney and the Faroes. It appears to have been compiled between 1387 and 1394. In it is a tale that purports to date from the eleventh century. The Norwegian poet, Sneglu-Halli, visits the court of King Harold Godwinson where he recites a special type of poem (a *dróttkvætt*) in honour of the English king. The Old Norse poetic form known as *dróttkvætt* (meaning 'lordly verse') added internal rhymes and use of similar vowel-sounds or the repetition of consonant sounds to an already complex genre of alliterative poetry. The joke in this case is that the Old English-speaking king does not understand the Old Norse of the poem.

When Sneglu-Halli returns to Norway, his own lord, King Harald Hardrada, asks him if he has ever recited poetry in honour of other kings. Sneglu-Halli replies that he recited one for 'the earl' (clearly a slight against King Harold Godwinson) but that it was a terrible poem. He adds that even a Danish poet could not have composed a worse one! (Clearly a slight aimed at Danes.) This same tale of an insult disguised as a praise-poem also appears in *Morkinskinna*, but there we are told that the poem was total nonsense and that Sneglu-Halli made it up on the spot.[4] Again, Harold Godwinson was none the wiser. And his own court poet told him that it was a good poem! The implication being that, like his king, he could not understand it either.

Clearly, those who later enjoyed this story in Iceland or Scandinavia were well aware of the tragic engagement of Harald Hardrada with the English king and so this jibe at the latter was made all the more bitter-sweet by the realization that he would ultimately be the one who would kill the King of Norway, before meeting his own death that same year at the Battle of Hastings. Whether an Old Norse poem would really have been unintelligible to a well-educated Old English-speaker in a court that was very well connected with Norse culture is a moot point, but it makes for a good story. It has been argued that 'Viking Age England was a bilingual society, but not a society comprised of bilingual individuals...'.[5] In other words, there was effective communication across the two communities (Old English and Norse) on the basis of mutually understood individual words and phrases but that is not the same as fluent bilingualism. So, maybe Harold Godwinson would not have fully understood what Sneglu-Halli was saying when it was couched in complex Norse poetry. But then again, Harold was raised in an Anglo-Danish context, so the whole Sneglu-Halli incident might be a later invention that does not shed any light on the actual linguistic abilities of the English court in 1066.

In contrast to the Norman chroniclers, later Scandinavian writers understandably put the Battle of Stamford Bridge centre-stage in their retelling of the events of 1066. Given its pivotal role in the eventual triumph of the Normans there is indeed a great deal to justify this attitude towards this battle. As *Haralds saga Sigurðarsonar* (*The Saga of Harald Sigurtharson* [Hardrada]) laconically puts it:

King Harold, the son of Godwin, gave permission to Óláf, the son of Harald Sigurtharson, to leave the country with the men who had not fallen in the battle. But he himself and his army marched to southern England, because the news had come to him just then that William the Bastard had invaded England in the south, taking possession of the land.[6]

This royal saga is one of many compiled by the Icelandic historian Snorri Sturluson, who died in 1241. The Scandinavian entanglement with England after the Norman Conquest is also reflected in later sagas and histories. Snorri Sturluson's *Magnúss saga Berfætts* (*Saga of Magnús Barelegs*, also found in *Heimskringla*, Snorri's history of the kings of Norway) records a clash between Magnus III (King of Norway between 1093 and 1103) and Norman lords operating in northern Wales as part of the Norman expansion into Wales, which clashed with Norwegian ambitions in the Irish Sea area:

> Then King Magnús steered his fleet to Bretland [Wales]. And when he arrived at the Sound of Anglesey [Menai Strait] a fleet approached from Bretland, headed by two earls, Hugh the Proud and Hugh the Stout, and at once gave battle. It was a hard fight.[7]

According to Snorri, Earl Hugh the Proud was killed when an arrow, fired by King Magnus himself, struck him in the eye. The twelfth-century poem *Magnússdrápa* (*Drápa* – a long series of poetic stanzas – *about Magnús*) by the (probably) Icelandic poet, Bjorn krepphendi (the Crooked-handed) dramatically describes how:

> ...the arrow-point flew fast where weapons soared. The slayer of the Jótar [Magnus] has advanced throughout all the islands with the sword for some time; far and wide the earth is controlled by the retainers of the worthy ruler.[8]

The Norman earl referred to as Hugh the Proud (*Hugi inn prúði* in Old Norse) was Hugh of Montgomery, Earl of Shrewsbury, while Hugh the Stout (*Hugi inn digri* in Old Norse) was Hugh of Avranches, Earl of Chester. The battle is commemorated in other Scandinavian sources too, although there are disagreements about who fired the fatal arrow and which of the Hughs was killed. One account says another bowman was responsible for the Norman earl's death but then threw his bow to Magnus and dedicated the shot to him. This confusion may explain why Snorri describes it as being '*konunginum kennt*' ('attributed to the king'), which leaves some room for doubt over whether Magnus himself actually fired the fatal arrow.[9] The Welsh writer known as Gerald of Wales (*Giraldus Cambrensis*), writing his *Itinerarium Cambriae* (*Journey through Wales*) in 1191, identified the dead Norman as Hugh of Chester ('*comes Hugo Cestrensis*' in Gerald's Latin account).

All of this reminds us (as we have seen in this book) that the Viking involvement in England that led to 1066 was far from over in that year and that Scandinavian entanglements continued and were reflected in Norse literature far beyond that date. We should, therefore, avoid the compartmentalizing of history that separates out the 'Norman Conquest' from the complex web of entanglements of the Viking Wars and the intertwining of the history of England with Scandinavia and the wider Viking-derived world (including Normandy).

England and Scandinavia: an ongoing connection

Even as late as the end of the twelfth century echoes of this entanglement continued to influence royal marriage policies and ambitions on the other side of the English Channel. In 1193, King Philip II of France married Ingeborg of Denmark as part of his manoeuvring against King John of England. Ingeborg was the daughter of the previous Danish king and the sister of the current one, Cnut VI. The marriage gave Philip a claim to the English throne through the old Danish claim that had not entirely been forgotten, even as late as the 1190s 'and also a strong fleet and army, offering the prospect of a two-pronged attack on England. This combination did for Harold in 1066.'[10]

The old Viking-English-French connection seemed about to reassert itself. Historical *déjà vu* was on the agenda, with the prospect of a cross-Channel invasion coinciding with a Scandinavian descent on England from across the North Sea. Consequently, 1193 looked like it was about to become a re-run of 1066. However, it was not to be. For reasons that are now lost to us, Philip repudiated his wife the day after their wedding and in one action the alliance with Denmark broke down and Philip fell out with the papacy too, since the Pope upheld the validity of the marriage. Poor Ingeborg refused to go quietly back to Denmark and Philip imprisoned her, marrying his mistress in 1196. So, 1066 was not repeated.

However, the echo of past events had not quite died away for, in 1213, Philip finally released Ingeborg – just at a time when he was once again considering an invasion of England and once again wanted Denmark on-side. Once again, echoes of past events can be heard in this action. Once again, a planned invasion of England from the direction of France was reliant on events in Scandinavia. But it was to be the last time that this nexus was to operate, and by the time that the French invasion actually occurred (in 1216) it was no longer dependent on the Scandinavian connection. The echoes of the 1066 Viking connection had finally faded to silence, but not before they had reminded us of the importance of that original combination of factors that led to the Norman Conquest. And these original factors had themselves been rooted in the often overlooked consequences of the 'Viking Conquest' of 1016.

As we have seen in this book, the 'Viking Conquest' of 1016 led to 1066 more than any other factor. It led to a close and ongoing dynastic connection with Scandinavia. It destabilized, broke up and re-configured the English political landscape. It left numerous Scandinavian kings with claims (of varying degrees of persuasiveness) to the English throne. It was the root of the enmity between Edward the Confessor and the Godwins. It led to the Norman claim to the throne (rooted in a relationship that predated 1016 and which was itself caused by the Viking Wars). It marginalized the legitimate heirs to the English throne. It made possible the rise of non-royal contenders for the throne. It led to the Norwegian invasion of 1066 that helped William win at Hastings. Finally, Scandinavian interventions after 1066 were a major reason why the Norman Conquest developed in the way that it did. It is therefore justifiable to say that '1016' led to '1066': the Vikings caused the Norman Conquest.

Notes

Chapter 1. '1066 and All That': So What?

[1] Williams, A. and Martin, G.H. (eds), *Domesday Book: A Complete Translation* (Penguin, London, 2003), p.409.

[2] Wood, M., *Domesday: A Search for the Roots of England* (BBC Publications, London, 1986), p.39.

[3] Morris, M., *The Norman Conquest* (Hutchinson, London, 2012), pp.230–31.

[4] Palliser, D.M., 'Domesday Book and the "harrying of the north"', *Northern History*, 29 (1993), pp.9–10.

[5] Dalton, P., *Conquest, Anarchy and Lordship: Yorkshire, 1066-1154* (Cambridge University Press, Cambridge, 2002), p.24.

[6] Dalton, P., *ibid*, p.25, quoting the work of W.E. Wightman, 'The significance of "waste" in the Yorkshire Domesday', *Northern History*, 10 (1975), pp.55–71.

[7] Morris, M., *The Norman Conquest*, p.230.

[8] Whittock, M., *A Brief History of Life in the Middle Ages* (Constable and Robinson, London, 2009), p.173.

Chapter 2. 1016: The 'Forgotten Conquest'

[1] For an overview of the Viking Wars in their entirety and the impact of the Vikings on England and the British Isles see: Whittock, M., and Whittock, H., *The Viking Blitzkrieg AD789–1098* (History Press, Stroud, 2013) for the Vikings Wars in England; and Carroll, J., Harrison, S. and Williams, G., *The Vikings in Britain and Ireland* (British Museum Press, London, 2014) for the impact on the British Isles. The latter book accompanied the major British Museum exhibition on the Vikings in 2014.

[2] To explore the importance of Edgar, see Rex, P., *Edgar: King of the English 959–75* (Tempus, Stroud, 2007).

[3] To explore more of the reign of Æthelred II, see Williams, A., *Æthelred the Unready: the Ill-Counselled King* (Hambledon Continuum, London, 2003); and Lavelle, R., *Aethelred II, King of the English* (The History Press, Stroud, 2008).

[4] Haywood, J., *The Penguin Historical Atlas of the Vikings* (Penguin Books, London, 1995), p.108.

[5] Williams, G. and Graham-Campbell, J. (eds), *Silver Economy in the Viking Age* (Left Coast Press Inc., Walnut Creek, California, 2007).

[6] Hunter Blair, P. and Keynes, S., *An Introduction to Anglo-Saxon England* (Cambridge University Press, Cambridge, 3rd edn, 2003), pp.96–7.

[7] See Snorrason, O. and Andersson, T.M. (transl.), *The Saga of Olaf Tryggvason* (Cornell University Press, Ithaca, New York, 2003).

[8] Downham, C., 'England and the Irish-Sea Zone in the eleventh century', in Gillingham, J. (ed.), *Anglo-Norman Studies XXVI: Proceedings of the Battle Conference 2003* (Boydell Press, Woodbridge, 2004), pp.59–60.

[9] A succinct summary by Professor Malcolm Godden, as well as the text and translation of the poem, can be found at: http://www.english.ox.ac.uk/oecoursepack/maldon/ (accessed December 2015).

[10] Warwick Frese, D., 'Poetic Prowess in Brunanburh and Maldon: Winning, Losing, and Literary Outcome' in Rugg Brown, P., Ronan Crampton, G. and Robinson, F.C. (eds), *Modes of Interpretation in Old English Literature* (University of Toronto Press, Toronto, 1986), pp.83–99.

[11] For an overview of some of the issues relating to the poem, see Cooper, J. (ed.), *The Battle of Maldon: Fiction and Fact* (Hambledon Continuum, London, 1993).

[12] Whitelock, D. (ed.), *English Historical Documents, Volume I, c.500–1042* (Eyre Methuen, London, 1979), p.324.

[13] Whitelock, D., *ibid.*, p.236.

[14] Whitelock, D., *ibid.*, p.239.

[15] Whitelock, D., *ibid.*, p.591.

[16] Howard, I., *Swein Forkbeard's Invasions and the Danish Conquest of England, 991–1017* (Boydell Press, Woodbridge, 2003), p.70.

[17] *British Archaeology*, July/August 2012, Number 125, p.8.

[18] Loe, L, 'Death on Ridgeway Hill: How Science unlocked the secrets of a mass grave', *Current Archaeology*, February 2015, issue 299, pp.38–43.

[19] Whitelock, D., *English Historical Documents*, p.239.

[20] Whitelock, D., *ibid.*, p.241.

[21] Stafford, P., *Unification and Conquest: Political and Social History of England in the Tenth and Eleventh Centuries* (Hodder Arnold, London, 1989), pp.64–5.

[22] Lapidge M., Blair, J., Keynes, S. and Scragg, D. (eds), *The Blackwell Encyclopaedia of Anglo-Saxon England* (Blackwell Publishing, Oxford, 1999), pp.150–51.

[23] Whitelock, D., *English Historical Documents*, p.243.

[24] Bradbury, I., *The Battle of Hastings* (Sutton Publishing, Stroud, 1998), p.14.

[25] Whitelock, D., *English Historical Documents*, p.245.

[26] Page, R.I., *Reading the Past: Runes* (British Museum Publications, London, 1987), p.46.

[27] http://www.britannica.com/topic/Danegeld

[28] Graham-Campbell, J., *The Viking World* (Frances Lincoln Limited, London, 2001), p.164.

[29] Lawson, M.K., 'The Collection of Danegeld and Heregeld in the Reigns of Aethelred II and Cnut', *The English Historical Review*, Vol. 99, No. 393 (Oct., 1984), pp.721–38.

[30] Page, R.I., *Reading the Past: Runes*, p.46.

Chapter 3. New King ... New Broom ...

[1] Campbell, A. (ed.), *Encomium Emmae Reginae*, Camden 3rd series 72 (Royal Historical Society, London, 1949), pp.15–16.

[2] Williams, A., 'Thorkell the Tall and the bubble reputation: the vicissitudes of fame', http://www.academia.edu/1682316/, p.11 (accessed November 2015).

[3] Whitelock, D., Douglas, D.C. and Tucker, S.I. (trans and eds), *The Anglo-Saxon Chronicle: A Revised Translation* (Eyre and Spottiswoode, London, 1961), p.97.

[4] McCully, C. and Hilles, S., *The Earliest English: An Introduction to Old English Language* (Pearson Education, Oxford, 2005), p.70; Bolton, T., *The Empire of Cnut the Great: Conquest and the Consolidation of Power in Northern Europe in the Early Eleventh Century* (Brill, Leiden, 2009), pp.43–44.

[5] Williams, A., 'Introduction', in Owen-Crocker, G.R. and Schneider, B.W., *Kingship, Legislation and Power in Anglo-Saxon England* (Boydell & Brewer, Woodbridge, 2013), p.10.

[6] Whitelock, D., Douglas, D.C. and Tucker, S.I., *The Anglo-Saxon Chronicle*, p.97.

[7] *Ibid.*, p.133.

[8] Whitelock, D. (ed.), *English Historical Documents, Volume I, c.500–1042* (Eyre Methuen, London, 1979), p.312.

[9] Williams, A., Smyth, A.P and Kirby, D.P., *A Biographical Dictionary of Dark Age Britain* (B.A. Seaby, London, 1991), p.115.

[10] Treasure, G. and Dawson, I., *Who's Who in British History: A–H* (Taylor & Francis, Abingdon, 1998), p.1207.

[11] Harper-Bill, C. and Van-Houts, E., *A Companion to the Anglo-Norman World* (Boydell & Brewer, Woodbridge, 2007), pp.7–8.

[12] Lawson, M.K., *Cnut: England's First Viking King* (Tempus, Stroud, 1993), p.84.

[13] *Ibid.*, p.86.

Chapter 4. New Men and New Opportunities

[1] Barlow, F., *Edward the Confessor* (Yale University Press, New Haven and London, 2nd edn, 1997), p.54.

[2] Wulfstan, *Sermo Lupi ad Anglos*, in Whitelock, D. (ed.), *English Historical Documents, Vol. I, c.500–1042* (Eyre Methuen, London, 1979), p.56.

[3] Barlow, F., *Edward the Confessor*, p.55.

[4] Whitelock, D. (ed.), *English Historical Documents, Vol. I, c.500–1042* (Eyre Methuen, London, 1979), p.242.

[5] John, E., 'Edward the Confessor and the Norman Succession', *Historical Review* (1979) XCIV (CCCLXXI), p.244.

[6] Barlow, F., *The Godwins: the Rise and Fall of a Noble Dynasty* (Routledge, Harlow, 2002), p.33.

[7] Baxter, S., 'MS C of the Anglo-Saxon Chronicle and the Politics of Mid-Eleventh-Century England', *English Historical Review* 122 (2007), p.1198.

[8] *Ibid.*, p.1224.

[9] *Ibid.*, p.1215.

[10] *Ibid.*, p.1224.

[11] Lund, N., 'Cnut's Danish Kingdom', in Rumble, A.R. (ed.), *The reign of Cnut: King of England, Denmark and Norway*, (Leicester University Press, London, 1994), p.38.

[12] *Ibid.*, p.96.

[13] Saxo Grammaticus, *Danorum Regum* X. 16, Christensen, E. (ed. and trans.), BAR International Series, 84, pp.31–4.

[14] Lund, 'Cnut's Danish Kingdom', p.38.

[15] *Ibid.*, p.97.

[16] Sawyer, P.H., 'Cnut's Scandinavian Empire', with appendix by Sawyer, B., 'The evidence of Scandinavian runic inscriptions', in Rumble, A.R. (ed.), *The reign of Cnut: King of England, Denmark and Norway* (Leicester University Press, London, 1994), p.19.

[17] *Ibid.*, p.20.

[18] Campbell, M.W., 'Queen Emma and Ælfgifu of Northampton: Canute the Great's women', *Mediaeval Scandinavia* 4 (1971), pp.73–4.

[19] Lund, 'Cnut's Danish Kingdom', p.108.

[20] Campbell, 'Queen Emma', p.75.

[21] Townend, M., 'Like father, like son? Glælognskviða and the Anglo-Danish cult of saints', *Scandinavia and Christian Europe in the Middle Ages*, Papers of the Twelfth International Saga Conference, Bonn/Germany, 28 July–2 August 2003, Simek, R. and Meurer, J. (eds.) (Hausdruckerei der Universität Bonn, 2003), p.474.

[22] Ibid.

[23] *Ibid.*, p.475.

[24] Rollason, D.W., *Saints and Relics in Anglo-Saxon England* (Blackwell, Oxford, 1989), p.144.

[25] http://www.medievalhistories.com/dna-old-bones-cnut-great/, *6 February 2015* (accessed November 2015).

Chapter 5. Home Thoughts From Abroad: A Postcard From Normandy

[1] McGlynn, S., *Blood Cries Afar: The Magna Carta War and the Invasion of England 1215–1217* (The History Press, Stroud, 2015), p.143.

[2] Graham-Campbell, J. (ed.), *The Viking World* (Frances Lincoln, London, 2001), p.32.

[3] Morris, M., *The Norman Conquest* (Windmill Books, London, 2013), pp.48–9.

[4] See for example: Carson Pastan, E., White, S.D. and Gilbert, K., *The Bayeux Tapestry and Its Contexts: A Reassessment* (Boydell & Brewer, Woodbridge, 2014), p.242.

[5] Dudo of St Quentin says it was spoken there until at least the 930s and implies that Richard I of Normandy was a fluent speaker: Christiansen, E. (trans.), *Dudo of St Quentin, History of the Normans* (Boydell & Brewer, Woodbridge, 1998), pp.xvii–xviii.

[6] Sawyer, P. (ed.), *The Oxford Illustrated History of the Vikings* (Oxford University Press, Oxford, 1997), p.31.

[7] Graham-Campbell, J. (ed.), *The Viking World*, p.32.

[8] Bates, D., 'In search of the Normans', *BBC History Magazine*, volume 13, number 8, August 2012, p.33.

[9] Treasure, G. and Dawson, I., *Who's who in British History: A–H* (Routledge, London, 1998), p.426.

[10] Brown, R.A., *The Normans* (Boydell & Brewer, Woodbridge, 1994), p.16.

[11] Whitelock, D. (ed.), *English Historical Documents, Volume I, c.500–1042* (Eyre Methuen, London, 1979), p.237.

[12] Williams, A., Smyth, A.P. and Kirby, D.P., *A Biographical Dictionary of Dark Age Britain: England, Scotland, and Wales, c. 500–c.1050* (B.A. Seaby, London, 1991), p.28.

[13] Morris, M., *The Norman Conquest*, pp.16–17.

[14] Brown, R.A., *The Normans,* p.16.

[15] An interesting suggestion made by Barlow, F., *Edward the Confessor* (Yale University Press, New Haven & London, 1997, Yale edition), p.37.

[16] Barlow, F., *ibid.*, p.40.

[17] Morris, M., *The Norman Conquest*, p.20.

[18] Brown, R.A., *The Normans*, p.16.

[19] Lewis, P., 'The French in England before the Norman Conquest', *Anglo-Norman Studies* 17 (1995), p.123.

[20] Lewis, P., *ibid.*, pp.126–7.

Chapter 6. Sons and Lovers: Cnut's Two Marriages and his Competing Sons

[1] Campbell, A., *Encomium Emmae Reginae*, Camden 3rd series 72 (Royal Historical Society, London, 1949), p.33.

[2] Williams, A., *Kingship and Government in Pre-Conquest England, c.500–1066* (Palgrave Macmillan, Basingstoke, 1999), p.135.

[3] Whitelock, D., Douglas, D.C. and Tucker, S.I. (transl. and eds), *The Anglo-Saxon Chronicle: A Revised Translation* (Eyre and Spottiswoode, London, 1961), p.103.

[4] North, J., *English Hammered Coinage, Volume 1, Early Anglo-Saxon to Henry III, c.600–1272* (Spink & Son, London, 1994), p.39.

[5] Whitelock, D., Douglas, D.C. and Tucker, S.I., *The Anglo-Saxon Chronicle*, p.104.

[6] North, J., *English Hammered Coinage*, p.39.

[7] Whitelock, D., Douglas, D.C. and Tucker, S.I., *The Anglo-Saxon Chronicle*, p.104.

[8] Howard, I., *Harthacnut: The Last Danish King of England* (The History Press, Stroud, 2008), p.56.

[9] Becker, C.J., 'Studies in the Danish Coinage at Lund during the period c.1030–1046', in Blackburn, M.A.S. and Metcalf, D.M. (eds.), *Viking-Age Coinage in the Northern Lands*, 2 vols (BAR Internat. ser. 122, Oxford, 1981), p.459.

[10] North, J., *English Hammered Coinage*, p.39.

[11] See: Parker, P., *The Northmen's Fury: A History of the Viking World* (Vintage Books, New York, 2015), p.264.

[12] Howard, I., *Harthacnut: The Last Danish King of England* (The History Press, Stroud, 2008), p.109.

[13] Keynes, S., in Lapidge, M., Blair, J., Keynes, S. and Scragg, D., *The Blackwell Encyclopaedia of Anglo-Saxon England* (Blackwell, 2001), p.230.

[14] Whitelock, D., Douglas, D.C. and Tucker, S.I., *The Anglo-Saxon Chronicle*, p.105.

[15] Howard, I., *ibid.*, p.123.

[16] Whitelock, D., Douglas, D.C. and Tucker, S.I., *The Anglo-Saxon Chronicle*, p.105.

[17] Whitelock, D., Douglas, D.C. and Tucker, S.I., *ibid.*, p.106.

[18] Higham, N.J., *The Death of Anglo-Saxon England* (Sutton, 1997), p.222.

[19] Higham, N.J., *ibid.*

Chapter 7. Home Thoughts From Abroad: A Postcard From Hungary

[1] http://www.lrgaf.org/guide/q&a1.htm; *see also*: http://www.wwwestra.com/horses/history_travel.htm (accessed July 2015).

[2] http://www.sea-distances.org/ (accessed July 2015).

[3] Keynes, S., 'The Declining Reputation of Æthelred the Unready', in Pelteret, D. (ed.), *Anglo-Saxon History: A Basic Reading* (Garland Publishing, New York and London, 2000), p.159.

[4] Whitelock, D. (ed.), *English Historical Documents, Volume I, c.500–1042* (Eyre Methuen, London, 1979), p.251.

[5] Whitelock, D., *ibid.*, p.312.

[6] Whitelock, D., Douglas, D.C. and Tucker, S.I. (transl. and eds), *The Anglo-Saxon Chronicle* (Eyre and Spottiswoode, London, 1961), p.133.

[7] Gransden, A., *Historical Writing in England, c.550 to c.1307* (Routledge and Kegan Paul, London, 1974), pp.209–12.

[8] Most notably in Ronay, G., *The Lost King of England: The East European Adventures of Edward the Exile* (Boydell Press, Woodbridge, 1989).

[9] Arguments explored in Ronay, G., *ibid.*

[10] Whitelock, D., Douglas, D.C. and Tucker, S.I., *The Anglo-Saxon Chronicle*, p.129.

[11] Keene, C., *Saint Margaret, Queen of the Scots: A Life in Perspective* (Palgrave Macmillan, London, 2013), pp.28–9.

[12] Keene, C., *ibid.*, p.29.

[13] Keene, C., *ibid.*

Chapter 8. Happy Families, Unhappy King:
The Reign of Edward the Confessor

[1] A good overview of the process of royal succession, as well as why the Anglo-Saxon royal family was so prestigious, can be found in Barlow, F., *Edward the Confessor* (Yale University Press, New Haven & London, 1997 Yale edition), pp.54–5.

[2] Harrison, K., *The Framework of Anglo-Saxon History to AD900* (Cambridge University Press, Cambridge, 1976), p.92.

[3] Barlow, F., *Edward the Confessor*, p.75.

[4] Lewis, P., 'The French in England before the Norman Conquest', *Anglo-Norman Studies* 17 (1995), p.123.

[5] John, E., *Reassessing Anglo-Saxon England* (Manchester University Press, Manchester, 1996), p.168.

[6] Harper-Bill, C. and Van Houts, E., *A Companion to the Anglo-Norman World* (Boydell & Brewer, Woodbridge, 2007), pp.2–11.

[7] John, E., *Reassessing Anglo-Saxon England*, p.175.

[8] Barlow, F., *Edward the Confessor*, p.117.

[9] Whitelock, D., Douglas, D.C. and Tucker, S.I. (transl. and eds), *The Anglo-Saxon Chronicle* (Eyre and Spottiswoode, London, 1961), p.24.

[10] Quoted in Barlow, F., *Edward the Confessor*, p.84.

[11] Charter S.1006.

[12] Barlow, F., *Edward the Confessor*, p.159.

[13] McLynn, F., *1066: The Year of the Three Battles* (Pimlico, London, 1999), pp.15–16.

[14] Howarth, D.A., *1066: The Year of the Conquest*, (Penguin, London, 1981), pp.69–70.

[15] McLynn, F., *1066: The Year of the Three Battles*, p.15.

[16] John, E., *Reassessing Anglo-Saxon England*, p.180.

[17] Whitelock, D., Douglas, D.C. and Tucker, S.I., *The Anglo-Saxon Chronicle*, p.138.

[18] A good overview of claimants to the English throne in the late 1050s and early 1060s can be found in Barlow, F., *Edward the Confessor*, pp.219–20.

[19] Whitelock, D., Douglas, D.C. and Tucker, S.I, *The Anglo-Saxon Chronicle*, p.138.

[20] http://news.bbc.co.uk/1/hi/england/london/4489842.stm (accessed October 2015).

Chapter 9. 1066: The Viking Year?

[1] William of Poitiers, *Histoire de Guillaume de Conquérant*, R. Foreville (ed), (CHF, Paris, 1952), p.154.

[2] Beckerman, J.S., 'Succession in Normandy, 1087, and in England, 1066: the Role of Testamentary Custom', *Speculum* 47 (1972), p.246. See also Bradbury, J., *The Battle of Hastings* (Sutton, Stroud, 1998), pp.121–2.

[3] See Rex, P., *Harold II. The Doomed Saxon King* (The History Press, Stroud, 2005), p.178, for a defence of Harold's legitimate right to the throne.

[4] Walker, I.W., *Harold: The Last Anglo-Saxon King* (The History Press, Stroud, 1997), p.155.

[5] Walker, I.W., *Harold*, p.157.

[6] For a detailed examination of this invasion see: DeVries, K., *The Norwegian invasion of England in 1066* (Boydell Press, Woodbridge, 1999).

[7] Walker, I.W., *Harold*, p.176.

[8] Longford, E., *The Oxford Book of Royal Anecdotes* (Oxford University Press, Oxford, 1989), p.46.

[9] Shepherd Creasy, E., *The Fifteen Decisive Battles of the World* (Courier Corporation, North Chelmsford, Massachusetts, 2012), p.169.

[10] See Wace, *Le Roman de Rou*, A.J. Holden (ed.) (A.&J. Picard, Paris, 1970–73), ii, p.173, and John of Worcester, *The Chronicle of John of Worcester*, R.R. Darlington, P. McGurk (eds), J. Bray, P. McGurk (transl.) (Clarendon Press, Oxford, 1995), ii., p.604.

[11] Royal Armouries calculation on BBC 4 *Bullets, Boots and Bandages: How to Really Win at War*, Episode 2, 'Stealing a March', February 2013.

[12] It is noteworthy that the only warriors shown using two-handed axes on the Bayeux Tapestry are Anglo-Saxon warriors. See Bradbury, J., *The Battle of Hastings* (Sutton, Stroud, 1998),

pp.90–92. At the earlier battle at Stamford Bridge the same kind of battle-axe was described as a peculiarly Scandinavian weapon by the later historian Henry of Huntingdon. See Henry, Archdeacon of Huntingdon, *Historia Anglorum (History of the English People)*, D. Greenway (ed. and transl.) (Oxford Medieval Texts, Oxford, 1996). A more recent examination of the Viking origins of this broad-axe can be found in Stephenson, I.P., *Viking Warfare* (Amberley, Stroud, 2012), pp.59–62; also, he examines Cnut's role in the formation of the *huscarls* on pp.80–81.

Chapter 10. The Vikings Return!

[1] See Haigh, C. (ed.), *The Cambridge Historical Encyclopedia of Great Britain and Ireland* (Cambridge University Press, Cambridge, 1990), p.76 for an overview of how the ambitions of Scandinavian rulers, after 1066, fitted into the pattern of competition for the English throne that stretched back to the 1030s.

[2] Williams, A., *The English and the Norman Conquest* (Boydell & Brewer, Woodbridge, 1997), p.18.

[3] Williams, A., *ibid.*, pp.19–20.

[4] Williams, A., *ibid.*, pp.17–18.

[5] Whitelock, D., Douglas, D.C. and Tucker, S.I. (transl. and eds), *The Anglo-Saxon Chronicle* (Eyre and Spottiswoode, London, 1961), p.146.

[6] Garmonsway, G.N. (ed. and transl.), *The Anglo-Saxon Chronicle* (J. M. Dent & Sons Ltd, London, 1972), p.203, note 3.

[7] Whitelock, D., Douglas, D.C. and Tucker, S.I., *The Anglo-Saxon Chronicle*, p.148.

[8] Green, J.A., *The Aristocracy of Norman England* (Cambridge University Press, Cambridge, 1997), pp.63–4.

[9] Barlow, F., *The Godwins* (Pearson, Harlow, 2002), p.169.

[10] McLynn, F., *1066: The Year of the Three Battles* (Pimlico, London, new edn., 1999), pp.15–16; and Strickland, M., 'Military Technology and Conquest: the Anomaly of Anglo-Saxon England', in C. Harper-Bill (ed.), *Anglo-Norman studies XIX: proceedings of the Battle Conference*, 1996 (Boydell Press, Woodbridge, 1997), p.377.

[11] Howarth, D.A., *1066: The Year of the Conquest*, (Penguin, London, 1981), pp.69–70; and McLynn, F., *1066: The Year of the Three Battles*, p.15.

[12] Arnold, M., *The Vikings: Culture and Conquest* (Hambledon Continuum, London, 2006), p.128.

[13] Haywood, J., *The Penguin Historical Atlas of the Vikings* (Penguin Books, London, 1995), pp.126–7.

[14] Haywood, J., *ibid.*

[15] For an overview of the revolt of Hereward, see Rex, P., *Hereward: the Last Englishman* (Tempus, Stroud, 2007).

[16] Rex, P., *ibid.*

[17] Wareham, A., *Lords and Communities in Early Medieval East Anglia* (Boydell Press, Woodbridge, 2005), p.85.

[18] Whitelock, D., Douglas, D.C. and Tucker, S.I., *The Anglo-Saxon Chronicle*, p.151.

[19] The mid-twelfth-century *De Gestis Herwardi Saxonis* (The exploits of Hereward the Saxon), of Hugh Candidus.

[20] Mynors, R.A.B., Thomson, R.M. and Winterbottom, M. (eds and transl.), *William of Malmesbury De Gestis Regum Anglorum* (Oxford Medieval Texts, Oxford, 1998), ii, p.318.

[21] Whitelock, D., Douglas, D.C. and Tucker, S.I., *The Anglo-Saxon Chronicle*, p.157.

[22] According to the Danish chronicles; the *Anglo-Saxon Chronicle, manuscripts E and D*, date his death to 1076, Whitelock, D., Douglas, D.C. and Tucker, S.I., *The Anglo-Saxon Chronicle*, p.158.

[23] Graham-Campbell, J. (ed.), *The Viking World* (Frances Lincoln Limited, London, 3rd edn, 2001), p.35.

[24] *The Ecclesiastical History of Orderic Vitalis*, Chibnall, M. (ed.), 6 vols, (Oxford University Press, Oxford, 1969–80), ii, p.267.

[25] Orderic Vitalis, *ibid.*, iv, pp.52–3.

[26] Roffe, D., *Decoding Domesday* (Boydell Press, Woodbridge, 2007), pp.7–10.

[27] Roffe, D., *Domesday: the Survey and the Book* (Oxford University Press, Oxford, 2002).

Chapter 11. Pulling the Threads Together

[1] http://www.asnc.cam.ac.uk/resources/mpvp/wp-content/uploads/2013/02/Introduction-to-Skaldic-Poetry_Debbie-Potts.pdf (accessed September 2015).

[2] Quoted in Christiansen, E. (trans.), *Dudo of St Quentin, History of the Normans* (Boydell & Brewer, Woodbridge, 1998), pp.xvii, note 24.

[3] An overview of these Scandinavia traditions can be found in Ghosh, S., *Kings' Sagas and Norwegian History: Problems and Perspectives* (Brill, Leiden, 2011), p.121.

[4] Fjalldal, M., *Anglo-Saxon England in Icelandic Medieval Texts* (University of Toronto Press, Toronto, 2005), p.15.

[5] Townend, M., *Language and History in Viking Age England: Linguistic Relations Between Speakers of Old Norse and Old English* (Brepols N.V: Turnhout, 2002), p.195.

[6] Snorri Sturluson, Heimskringla, *The Saga of Harald Sigurtharson (Hardruler)*, Hollander, L.E. (trans.), *Heimskringla, History of the Kings of Norway* (University of Texas Press, Austin, 1964), p.658.

[7] Snorri Sturluson, Heimskringla, *The Saga of Magnús Barelegs*, Hollander, L.E. (trans.), *Heimskringla, History of the Kings of Norway*, p.676.

[8] For the poem, its translation and commentary on it see: Kari Ellen Gade, Tarrin Wills, https://www.abdn.ac.uk/skaldic/m.php?p=verse&i=1910 (accessed August 2015).

[9] For a succinct overview of the incident as recorded in the surviving written sources, see Kari Ellen Gade, Tarrin Wills, *ibid.*

[10] McGlynn, S., *Blood Cries Afar: The Magna Carta War and the Invasion of England 1215–1217* (The History Press, Stroud, 2015), p.67.

Index